chapter 1

Where Do Words Come From?

nglish has more words than any other language. Some word experts estimate that there may be as many as a million words in the English language. That's far more than French, Russian, and German put together! When William Shakespeare was writing his famous plays about 400 years ago, there were fewer than 50,000 words in the English language. Now there are many, many times that. Where did all these words come from? They came from a lot of different sources.

Other Languages

When you speak English, you speak words from at least a hundred different languages, probably more. Some authorities believe that practically every language of the world has contributed something to English.

Here are some examples of everyday words that came from other languages.

From Greek:
  alphabet, drama, hippopotamus

From Spanish:
  fiesta, patio, rodeo

From Latin:
  camera, family, umbrella

From German:
  pretzel, sauerkraut, waltz

From French:
  bureau, fiancée, resumé

From Italian:
  graffiti, pasta, solo

From Native American languages:
  pecan, skunk, tomato

From African languages:
  banjo, gumbo, okra

In the following passage, there are words from 24 different languages. Can you spot them?

A robot in his pajamas was eating goulash and shish kebab and playing the piano, while a walrus looked out the window at a poodle strumming the ukulele under a bamboo tree. A dentist poured ketchup on his yogurt as a kid rode around on a unicorn. With his eight arms, an octopus on an iceberg was demonstrating karate chops, while an aardvark taught a moose algebra, and an alligator read his favorite magazine and shouted, "Hallelujah!"

How many did you find? Here they are:

robot: Czech

pajamas: Persian

goulash: Hungarian

shish kebab: Turkish

piano: Italian

walrus: Dutch

window: Old Norse

poodle: German

ukulele: Hawaiian

bamboo: Malay

dentist: French

ketchup: China

yogurt: Turkish

kid: Scandinavian

unicorn: Latin

octopus: Greek

iceberg: Danish/Norwegian

karate: Japanese

aardvark: Afrikaans

moose: Algonquin

algebra: Arabic

alligator: Spanish

magazine: Arabic

Hallelujah: Hebrew

If you'd like to play a vocabulary-building game with English words from foreign languages, turn to pages 143–144.

How to Tell What Language a Word Came From

Some dictionaries tell you what language a word came from in a special "Word History" or "History" box.

hel • i • cop • ter

Word History
• •

The French word *hélicoptère* was borrowed into English as **helicopter**. The French word comes from the Greek *heliko*, which is a form of *helix*, which means "spiral," and *pteron*, which means "wing."

Scholastic Children's Dictionary © 1996 by Scholastic Inc.

Some dictionaries put brackets **[ ]** around the word histories and use words like *Irish Gaelic* or *Old Portuguese* to tell you which language a word came from. Other dictionaries use abbreviations like the following:

Afr for African languages

Heb for Hebrew

Amerlnd for American Indian
  languages

Ind for Indian

Ar for Arabic

It for Italian

Chin for Chinese

Jp for Japanese

F for French

L for Latin

G for German

Russ for Russian

Gk for Greek

Span for Spanish

If you're not sure what an abbreviation means (*MDu*, for instance), look for a key or guide to the abbreviations. (*MDu* means "Middle Dutch.")

Amazingly, one word can come from many different languages. Take *delicatessen*, for instance. We all know that it means "a store or restaurant that sells cooked or prepared foods." But you will probably be surprised to learn that *delicatessen* came from

a German word, *delikatessen*, which came from
a French word, *délicatesse*, which came from
an Italian word, *delicatezza*, which came from
a Latin word, *delicatus*, which meant "pleasing."

Now that's something to chew on.

Eponyms: People and Places That Became Words

Sometimes a person does something so special that his or her name actually becomes a word. Sometimes something is created or becomes popular in a certain place, and the name of that place becomes the name of the thing. The people and places whose names become words are called *eponyms*.

WORDS THAT CAME FROM THE NAMES OF PEOPLE

Word	Meaning	Eponym	Reason
America	North, Central, and South America and the West Indies	Amerigo Vespucci (1454–1512) Italian navigator and explorer	A mapmaker named North and South America for Amerigo because he believed Vespucci's stories about his voyages to the New World, though they may not have actually been true.

WORDS THAT CAME FROM THE NAMES OF PEOPLE *(continued)*

Word	Meaning	Eponym	Reason
Braille	raised dots that stand for letters for blind readers	Louis Braille (1809–1852) teacher at a school for the blind in Paris	Braille published a system for printing books with raised dots in 1829.
Bunsen burner	a gas burner used in laboratories	Robert Bunsen (1811–1899) German chemist	Bunsen developed the first good laboratory burner. It produces a very hot flame.
cardigan	a sweater with a round or V neck that opens down the front	Lord Cardigan (James Brudenell) (1797–1868) British general	Cardigan wore this type of sweater and made it popular.
Celsius	a temperature scale that registers the freezing point of water as 0° and the boiling point as 100°	Anders Celsius (1701–1744) Swedish astronomer	In 1742, Celsius made up the Celsius temperature scale.
decibel	a measurement of the loudness of sounds	Alexander Graham Bell (1847–1922) American inventor	Bell invented the audiometer, an instrument for measuring sounds.

Word	Meaning	Eponym	Reason
diesel engine	an internal combustion engine	Rudolf Diesel (1858–1913) German mechanical engineer	Diesel invented this powerful engine to take the place of slower steam engines.
Fahrenheit	a temperature scale that registers the freezing point of water as 32° and the boiling point as 212°	Gabriel Daniel Fahrenheit (1686–1736) German physicist	Fahrenheit invented the mercury thermometer in 1714 and devised the Fahrenheit temperature scale.
Ferris wheel	an amusement park ride	George Washington Ferris (1859–1896) American inventor and engineer	Ferris designed a famous revolving wheel with cars as a ride at the 1893 World's Fair in Chicago.
Frisbee®	trademarked name for a plastic throwing disk	William Frisbie Founder, Frisbie Pie Co., Connecticut (1870s)	In the 1940s, people began throwing the Frisbie tin pie plates around for fun and the idea caught on.

WORDS THAT CAME FROM THE NAMES OF PEOPLE *(continued)*

Word	Meaning	Eponym	Reason
graham cracker	a cracker	Sylvester Graham (1794–1851) American clergyman, vegetarian	Graham invented this cracker of unsifted whole wheat flour, which he promoted as being healthful.
guy	a man; a fellow	Guy Fawkes (1560–1606) a man who tried to blow up the British Parliament	A dummy of Guy Fawkes is paraded through English towns and burned on Guy Fawkes Day, November 5. Over time, Guy came to mean "a man."
Jacuzzi®	trademarked name for a type of whirlpool bath	Roy Jacuzzi an inventor who worked for his 7 great-uncles' water pump company	In 1968, Roy designed and began selling the first self-contained whirlpool bathtub.
leotard	a tight, one-piece garment	Jules Léotard (1838–1870) French acrobat	Léotard designed this stretchable body-hugging garment for himself.
Levi's®	trademarked name for blue denim jeans	Levi Strauss (1829–1902) German immigrant	Levi Strauss made work pants for California gold miners. Now they're known as Levi's.

Word	Meaning	Eponym	Reason
maverick	an independent person who does not follow the group	**Samuel Maverick** cattle owner in Texas in the 1800s	Maverick didn't brand his cows, so those that strayed from the herd were on their own.

Morse code	beeps or flashes of light that represent letters	**Samuel F.B. Morse** (1791–1872) American inventor and painter	Morse devised this system of communication and in 1844 sent the first message from Washington to Baltimore.
pants	trousers	**Pantaloon** funny character in Italian comedies in the 1400s	The actor who played Pantaloon always wore red trousers, called pantaloons, later shortened to *pants*.

WORDS THAT CAME FROM THE NAMES OF PEOPLE (continued)

Word	Meaning	Eponym	Reason
pasteurized milk	milk that has been heated to kill germs	Louis Pasteur (1822–1895) French scientist	Pasteur developed a way to destroy germs in food by heating, then chilling, it.
peach Melba	raspberry sauce over peaches and ice cream	Dame Nellie Melba (1861–1931) Australian opera singer	A famous French chef created this special dessert for one of Ms. Melba's parties.
sandwich	food between two pieces of bread	The Fourth Earl of Sandwich (1718–1792) British lord	The earl ordered his servant to wrap his meat in bread so that he could eat while playing cards.
saxophone	a wind instrument popular with jazz musicians	Antoine Joseph Sax (1814–1894) Belgian instrument maker	Sax invented the instrument and first played it in Paris in 1844.
sideburns	whiskers down the sides of the face	General Ambrose Burnside (1824–1881) Union general in the Civil War; political leader	Burnside's picture was often in the papers, and his famous facial whiskers were named sideburns (Burnside switched around) after him.

Word	Meaning	Eponym	Reason
teddy bear	a small, stuffed toy bear	Theodore Roosevelt nickname "Teddy" (1858–1919), the 26th President of the United States	Roosevelt would not kill a baby bear while on a hunting trip, so manufacturers called toy bears "teddy bears" in tribute to him.
vandal	a destroyer of property	Vandals a fierce Germanic tribe	The Vandals destroyed Rome in A.D. 455.
volt	a unit of electrical force	Alessandro Volta (1745–1827) Italian physicist	Volt invented the first electric battery in 1800.
Washington, D.C.	the capital city of the United States	George Washington (1732–1799) Revolutionary War commander; first President of the United States	The city was named in honor of this famous American hero. So was the state of Washington.

WORDS THAT CAME FROM THE NAMES OF PLACES

Word	Meaning	Eponym	Reason
bikini	a two-piece bathing suit	Bikini atoll a little island in the Pacific Ocean	In 1946, the United States began testing atom bombs on Bikini atoll. In the same year the little bathing suit was shown in Paris and named after the island.
bologna or baloney	a seasoned, smoked, mixed-meat sausage	Bologna a city in northern Italy	Bologna, Italy, became famous for its delicious sausage, which is named after the city.
cheddar	a smooth, hard cheese	Cheddar a village in southwestern England	This mild-to-sharp cheese was first made in the village of Cheddar.
frankfurter	a smoked-meat sausage	Frankfurt a city in Germany	Hot dogs first came from this German city.
hamburger	a patty made of ground meat	Hamburg a city in Germany	Hamburgers were first cooked and eaten in this German city.
jeans	pants made of heavy cotton	Genoa a city in northwestern Italy	The strong cloth for these pants was first woven in this city.

Word	Meaning	Eponym	Reason
marathon	a 26-mile race	**Marathon** a plain in ancient Greece	A messenger ran 26 miles from Marathon to Athens to give news of a victory in a battle in 490 B.C.
tuxedo	a man's dress suit used for special occasions	**Tuxedo Park,** New York	A new-style dark, formal suit was first worn to a ball in this town in the late 1800s.

Made-Up Words

Writers, poets, playwrights, journalists, songwriters, and speakers often make up words to fit special situations or to name something new. If enough people begin using these words, they become part of our language and are put into dictionaries.

Reduplications: Fun Words

Sometimes writers and speakers take words and add sounds that rhyme or nearly rhyme, or they double the sounds of words. The new words are called reduplications because the second part of the word duplicates, or copies, the sound of the first part. Here are some reduplications that people use every day.

Rhyming Words

bigwig
an important person

boogie-woogie
fast jazz piano playing

boo hoo
sound of crying

bow-wow
sound a dog makes

claptrap
worthless language

even-steven
nothing owed on
either side

fuddy-duddy
a fussy person

fuzzy-wuzzy
very soft

handy-dandy
clever with hands

harum-scarum
reckless and hasty

heebie-jeebies
jumpy feeling

helter-skelter
hasty, confused,
careless

higgledy-piggledy
confused and
disorderly

hobnob
to be on friendly
terms

hocus-pocus
magic trick/words

hodgepodge
a mess of junk

hoi polloi
ordinary people

hoity-toity
snooty, snobby

hokeypokey
a group dance

holy moly
a cry of surprise

hubbub
uproar, turmoil

hully-gully
a group dance

humdrum
boring, monotonous

hunky-dory
fine, satisfactory

hurdy-gurdy
a musical instrument

hurly-burly
noisy commotion

itsy-bitsy or itty-bitty
very, very small

jeepers creepers
a cry of surprise or
dismay

kowtow
to be obedient and
submissive to

lovey-dovey
very affectionate

mumbo jumbo
gibberish

namby-pamby
cowardly or weak

nitty-gritty
heart of the matter

okey-dokey
OK or okay

ragtag
disorderly, shaggy

razzle-dazzle
showy excitement

razzmatazz
flashy double-talk

rinky-dink
inferior, cheap

roly-poly
short and pudgy

rootin'-tootin'
enthusiastic

superduper
terrific, marvelous,
great

teeny-weeny
very, very small

tutti-frutti
with many fruit
flavors

wheeler-dealer
a person who makes
big deals

willy-nilly
without a plan;
wanted or not

wingding
a lavish, lively party

Almost-Rhyming Words

chitchat
small talk, gossip

clickety-clack
the sound a train
makes

clippety-clop
the sound of a
horse's hooves

dillydally
to waste time, dawdle

dingdong
the sound of a bell
ringing

doodad
a gadget or trinket

fiddle-faddle
nonsense, stupidity

flimflam
fraud, swindle, tricks

flip-flop
a sudden reversal

flippety-flop
sound of motion or
something flapping

gobbledygook
unclear, meaningless
talk

hee-haw
donkey sound; loud
laugh

hippety-hop
sound of an animal
moving

ho-hum
dull, boring

hunky-dory
fine, good, all right

jibber-jabber
nonsense words

jingle-jangle
sound of metal pieces
touching

knickknack
a small, fancy
ornament

lickety-split
very fast

mishmash
a mix of unrelated
stuff

Ping-Pong
trademarked name
for table tennis game

pitter-patter
rapid light tapping
sounds

riffraff
people with bad
reputations

seesaw
a teeter-totter

shilly-shally
to hesitate, delay,
waver

splish-splash
liquid hitting a
surface

telltale or tattletale
a person who tells
secrets

ticktock
the sound of a clock

tip-top
the best,
excellent

topsy-turvy
completely disordered

whippersnapper
small, insignificant
person

wishy-washy
weak-willed;
ineffective

zigzag
to turn sharply,
side to side

Double-Sound Words

bonbon
chocolate-covered
candy

boo-boo
an injury or mistake

buddy-buddy
very friendly

cancan
high-kicking French
dance

cha-cha
Latin American dance

goody-goody
extremely good or
sweet

ha-ha
the sound of laughter

huggy-huggy
very affectionate

hush-hush
secret, confidential

no-no
something you
shouldn't do

pom-pom
paper streamers
on a stick

pooh-pooh
to express dislike

rah-rah	tom-tom	yo-yo
enthusiastic, spirited	small-headed drum	toy spool on a string

so-so	tutu	yum-yum
average, passable	short ballet skirt	delicious

Portmanteau Words: Words Squished Together to Make New Words

Portmanteau is a French word for a large leather suitcase. Just as people squeeze clothes into their luggage, some clever speakers and writers squeeze parts of words together to create words that name something new.

For instance, when hotels were first built on highways, an imaginative person took bits of the words *motor* and *hotel* and combined them to make *motel*.

Here are some examples of common portmanteau words in English.

Word	Derivation	Meaning
BLOB	binary large object	a very large computer file
brunch	breakfast + lunch	a late-morning meal
byte	binary + table	a unit of computer information that represents a number or a letter
chortle	chuckle + snort	a snorting chuckle or happy laugh
clump	chunk + lump	a clustered mass; a lump
con man	confidence + man	a cheater or swindler

Word	Derivation	Meaning
emoticon	emotion + icon	a series of keyed characters used in e-mail to show emotions, such as :-) for pleasure, or :-(for sadness
flurry	flutter + hurry	a sudden commotion
fortnight	fourteen + nights	a period of two weeks
infomercial	information + commercial	a very long television commercial
modem	modulator + demodulator	a computer/telephone device
moped	motor + pedal	a lightweight motorized bicycle
motorcade	motor + cavalcade	a procession of motor vehicles
netiquette	Internet + etiquette	polite behavior over the Internet
pixel	picture + element	the smallest unit of a video picture
skylab	sky + laboratory	a large laboratory in space
slanguage	slang + language	language with a lot of slang
smash	smack + mash	to break into pieces violently
smog	smoke + fog	air pollution caused by fog and smoke

splatter	spl**ash** + s**p**atter	to scatter, splash, soil, and spatter
splotch	sp**ot** + b**lot** + bot**ch**	a spot, stain, or discolored area
squiggle	squ**irm** + wr**iggle**	a small, wiggly mark or scrawl
telethon	tele**phone** + mara**thon**	a long TV show that raises money
twirl	tw**ist** + wh**irl**	to swing in a circle, revolve briskly

New Words and Expressions

Hundreds of new words and expressions are added to English every year. New words, new expressions, and new meanings for old words come from many different places.

Popular Culture (entertainment, fashion, books, newspapers)

> **hip-hop** A style of music, poetry, dancing, art, and dress that originated in urban areas and whose popularity spread worldwide.

Medicine

> **acid reflux** A new way to describe heartburn, a burning feeling in the chest caused by acidic stomach fluids flowing back.

Technology

> **V-chip** A computer chip in a television set that allows parents to block programs they think are unsuitable for their children.

Computers

> **dot-com** (pronunciation of ".com") Relating to a company that does business on the Internet.

Science

> **genome** The full set of genetic information a person inherits from his or her parents, including DNA located in chromosomes.

Business

> **greentailing** Selling products that do the least damage to the environment or that increase the ecological awareness of buyers.

Slang

> **yadda yadda yadda** Boring, unimaginative, unimportant, endless talk.

News and World Events

> **glasnost** (Russian) An official policy of a government that allows freer discussion of issues than before.

Here is a batch of words and expressions that probably weren't in any dictionaries when you were born, but they are now.

> **actioner** A movie with lots of fast-moving action.
> **chatroom** A site on the Internet where many people carry on on-line conversations at the same time.
> **chiphead** Somebody who loves using computers.
> **cookie** Information (name, date, time, etc.) stored on a computer, used by Web sites to identify users of that Web site.

cyberpunk Action-packed science-fiction stories that are about future societies based on computers.

digerati People who have, or claim to have, very advanced skills in computers, the Internet, and the World Wide Web.

download To receive a file sent over a computer network.

dream team A group of experts in a certain field gathered together to give advice or solve a problem.

e-commerce Buying and selling goods and services on the Internet.

gazillion A tremendously large number of something.

Generation Y People who were born in the United States in the early 1980s to the late 1990s.

gonk To lie or exaggerate, especially on-line.

HOV ("high occupancy vehicle") lane A highway lane that is restricted during rush hours to vehicles with a minimum of two people.

keypal A person who exchanges a lot of e-mail with others.

LOL "Laughing out loud" (used in e-mail messages).

no-fly-zone (slang) A topic that must not be discussed.

nose stud A small, decorative button worn in a hole pierced in a person's nostril.

phone tag An exchange of phone calls in which messages are recorded but no conversation is achieved.

shiss The scratchy sound coming from the earphones of someone listening to a portable music player on high volume.

shopaholic Someone who can't resist shopping.

spam E-mail you didn't ask for that tries to sell you something.

strip mall A row of stores with a parking lot next to a road.

SUV (sport-utility vehicle) A roomy, four-wheel-drive vehicle designed for driving on unpaved roads.

zine (short for magazine) A cheaply produced underground publication.

EXTRA

Just a few years ago, nobody would have known what the following paragraph meant, but after reading this chapter, you should understand every word.

After playing phone tag with his friend, Sy Burr, a Generation Y'er, checked his e-mail only to find a lot of spam, so he went into a chatroom to see if his friend was there. Both of them were chip-heads who exchanged a gazillion e-mails a day. They were polite netizens who practiced proper netiquette and never tried to gonk anyone. All the yadda yadda yadda that Sy downloaded gave him acid reflux, but his keypal sent him a joke that made him LOL, so he sent back an emoticon of a smile.

chapter 2

Parts of Words

Prefixes, Roots, and Suffixes

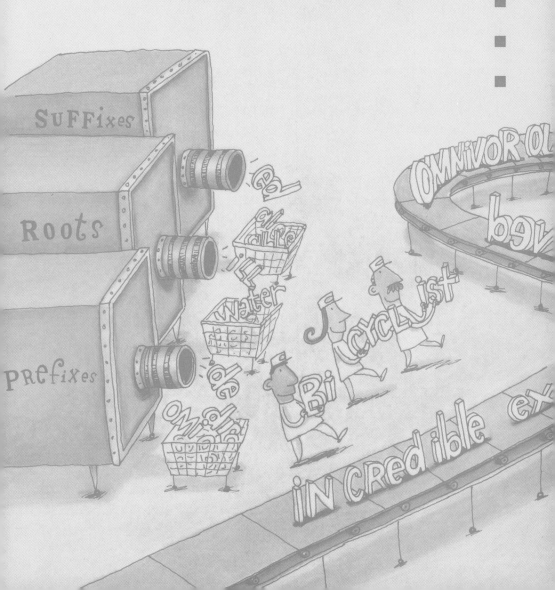

When a chef creates a great meal, he or she starts with certain ingredients, stirs in other fixings, and adds a bit at the end.

It's the same with words. There are many words that have a main part (called a **root**), a part added to the beginning of the root (called a **prefix**), and a part added to the end of the root (called a **suffix**). That combination can make for a very tasty word.

If you get to know what these prefixes, roots, and suffixes mean, you can figure out the definitions of many words without a dictionary.

For instance, think about the word **somnambulist**. If you know that

the prefix **somn-** means "sleep,"
the root **ambul** means "to walk," and
the suffix **-ist** means "a person who"

you might guess that **somnambulist** means "sleepwalker," and you'd be right!

What follows is a parade of the most-used word parts in our language.

PREFIXES

> **Prefix:** a part of a word that comes in front of the root and changes its meaning

Here are some of the most popular prefixes in English, along with a bunch of words that have those prefixes.

Note: The hyphen (-) after the prefix shows that it is not a whole word, only the beginning, and that part of the word comes after it.

Prefixes	Prefix Meanings	Sample Words and Definitions
a-	on	afire on fire ashore on the shore aside on the side
ab- abs-	from, away, off	abduct carry away by force abnormal away from normal, not normal absent away, not present
ambi-	both	ambidextrous able to use both hands equally well ambiguous having more than one meaning ambivalence conflicting or opposite feelings, such as love and hate, toward a person or thing
ante-	before, in front	antecede to come before something in time antemeridian before noon anteroom a small room before the main room
anti-	against, opposite of	antibody a substance that destroys bacteria antiseptic a substance that prevents infection antislavery against slavery
aqu- aqua-	water	aquarium a container with water for fish aquatic relating to water aqueduct a pipe for moving water
arch-	chief, most important	archbishop the highest ranking bishop archduke nobleman with high rank, like a prince archenemy chief or worst enemy

Prefixes	Prefix Meanings	Sample Words and Definitions
astro-	star, stars, outer space	astronaut a person trained to travel in space astronomer someone who studies the stars astrophysics the study of celestial objects
auto-	self, same, one	autocrat one person who rules a country autograph a person's own signature automatic acting by itself
bene-	good, well	benefactor person who gives money to a cause beneficial producing a good effect benefit something that has a good effect
bi-	two, twice, once in every two	biannual happening twice a year bicolor having two colors binoculars optical device with two lenses
biblio-	book	bibliography a list of books used as sources bibliomania an extreme love of books bibliophile a person who loves or collects books
bio-	life, living matter	biography a life story written by another person biology the science that deals with life biosphere Earth's surface inhabited by living things
cent-	hundred, hundredth	centennial the 100th anniversary centimeter 1/100 of a meter century 100 years
circum-	around, about	circumnavigate to sail around circumscribe to draw around; to limit the power circumspect looking around; cautious

Prefixes	Prefix Meanings	Sample Words and Definitions
co-	with, together, joint	coauthor writer who writes with another author coeducation the education of males and females together
com- con-	together with, jointly	combat fighting between people combine to join or mix together concur to agree with someone
contra- contro-	against, contrary, opposite	contradict to argue against contrary not in agreement controversy disagreement
counter-	opposite, contrary, opposing	counteract to oppose the effects of an action countermand to cancel a previous order counteroffensive attack against an attack
de-	reduce down, remove	debase to reduce something in value or quality decelerate to slow down; to reduce speed dethrone to remove from power
dis-	do the opposite, exclude, absence of, not	disagree to have a different opinion disappear to stop being seen disassemble to undo something that's assembled
equi-	equal, equally	equidistant an equal distance from two points equity equal and fair treatment of everyon equivalent equal in value, meaning, effect, etc.
ex-	from, out, out of, away from	excavate to dig out exhale to breathe out extract to draw or pull out

Prefixes	Prefix Meanings	Sample Words and Definitions
extra-	outside, beyond	extracurricular outside the school curriculum extraordinary beyond ordinary extraterrestrial outside the Earth
fore-	in front of, previous, earlier	forebear ancestor forebode to give an advance warning of something bad
geo-	earth, soil, global	geography study of the earth's surface geology study of the structure of the earth geoponics the study of agriculture
giga-	a billion	gigabyte unit of computer storage space gigahertz unit of frequency (one billion Hz/sec) gigawatt unit of electric power (one billion watts)
hemi-	half, partial	hemicycle a semicircular structure hemisphere one half the earth hemistich half a line of poetry
hetero-	different, other	heterogeneous made up of unrelated parts heteronyms words with same spelling but different meanings: *dove* (bird) and *dove* (did dive)
homo-	like, alike, same	homogeneous of the same nature or kind homophones words with same sound but different spellings: *eight* and *ate*
hydr- hydro-	water, liquid, moisture	hydrate to add water to hydrophobia intense fear of water hydroponics the growing of plants in liquid

Prefixes	Prefix Meanings	Sample Words and Definitions
hyper-	too much, over, above	hyperactive very restless hypercritical too critical hypertension pressure above normal
il- im- in- ir-	not, without	illegal not legal impossible not possible inappropriate not appropriate
inter-	between, among, jointly	interact to act upon one another international involving two or more countries intersection place where roads come together
intra-	within, inside	intramural involving students within one school intrastate existing in one state intravenous inside or into a vein
intro-	into, inward	introduce to lead into the main part of something introspect to look into your thoughts and feelings introvert shy person who keeps within him/herself
magni- magna-	great	magnanimous kind and big-hearted magnificent grand, impressive magnify to make appear larger
mal-	bad, badly, abnormal, inadequate	malfunction to function imperfectly or badly malicious wicked, spiteful, mean malign to write or say bad things about someone
mega-	great, large, huge	megalopolis an area with many nearby cities megaphone a device that projects a loud voice megastructure huge building or other structure

Prefixes	Prefix Meanings	Sample Words and Definitions
micro-	very small, short, minute	microbe a very small living thing microchip a tiny wafer with an integrated circuit microscope a device to see very small things
mid-	middle	midriff the area between the chest and the waist midterm middle of a term in school midway halfway between
mis-	bad, badly, wrong, wrongly	misbehave to behave badly misprint an error in printing misquote to quote wrongly
mono-	one, single, alone	monochromatic having one color monologue a speech spoken by one actor alone monotheism belief in one god
multi-	many, more than one or two	multicolored having many colors multilingual fluent in more than two languages multiplex building with several movie theaters
non-	no, not, without	nondescript with no special characteristics nonfiction true, real, not made-up nonsense without sense
ob-	in the way, against	object to be against something obscure hard to understand obstruct something that is in the way
octa- octo-	eight	octagon a figure with 8 sides and 8 angles octogenarian person in his or her 80s octopus sea animal with 8 arms

Prefixes	Prefix Meanings	Sample Words and Definitions
omni-	all	omnipotent **with all the power** omniscient **knowing all things** omnivorous **eating all foods**
pan-	all, any, everyone	panacea **a cure for all diseases or problems** panorama **an all-around view** pantheism **the worship of all gods**
ped- pedi-	foot, feet	pedal **a lever pushed by the foot** pedestrian **a walker** pedicure **cosmetic treatment of feet and toes**
per-	through, throughout	permanent **lasting throughout all time** permeate **to spread throughout** persist **to continue for a long time**
poly-	many, more than one	polychrome **with many colors** polyglot **fluent in many languages** polygon **shape with 3 or more straight sides**
post-	after, later, behind	posthumous **happening after someone's death** postpone **to delay something until later** postscript **a message at the end of a letter**
pre-	earlier, before, in front of	preamble **a part in front of a formal document** prepare **to get ready in advance** prepay **to pay ahead of time**
pro-	before, in front of	prognosis **a prediction of what will happen** prologue **a passage before the main part** prophet **a person who foretells the future**

Prefixes	Prefix Meanings	Sample Words and Definitions
quad- quadr- quadri-	four	quadrant open space with buildings on 4 sides quadrennium period of 4 years quadruped a 4-footed animal
re-	again, back, backward	rebound to spring back again, recover rebuild to build again rewind to wind something backward
retro-	backward, back	retroactive relating to something in the past retrogress to go back to an earlier condition retrospect the remembering of past events
self-	of, for, or by itself	self-discipline the ability to discipline yourself self-respect respect for yourself selfish concerned only with your own interests
semi-	half, partial	semiannual every half year semicircle half a circle semiconscious partly conscious
somn- somni-	sleep	insomnia inability to fall asleep somniloquy talking in your sleep somnolent feeling sleepy
sub-	under, lower than, inferior to	submarine an underwater boat submerge to put underwater substandard inferior to accepted standards
super-	higher in quality or quantity	Superbowl the football game above all others superior above average, better in quality supersonic faster than the speed of sound

Prefixes	Prefix Meanings	Sample Words and Definitions
tele-	far, distant	telephone a device to talk to a distant person telescope a device to view distant objects television a device to receive pictures from afar
trans-	across, beyond, through	transcontinental across the continent transfer to move from one place to another transport to carry something across a space
tri-	three, once in every three, third	triangle a figure with 3 sides and 3 angles triathlon an athletic contest with 3 events tricycle a 3-wheel vehicle with pedals
ultra-	beyond, extreme, more than	ultrahigh extremely high ultramodern more modern than anything else ultrasonic sound waves beyond human hearing
un-	not, opposite of, lacking	unabridged not shortened; full length unfair opposite of fair, just, and impartial unfriendly lacking friendliness; hostile
uni-	one, single	unicycle a vehicle with one wheel unilateral decided by only one person or nation unique the only one of its kind
vice-	acting in place of, next in rank	vice president the person next in rank to the president viceroy a governor who acts for a king or queen

ROOTS

Root: the main part of the word, which contains the basic meaning

Here are some of the most popular roots in English, along with a bunch of words that have those roots.

Roots	Root Meanings	Sample Words and Definitions
act	do	activity something that a person does react to do something in response transact to do business, carry on, do
aer aero	air	aerate to let air reach something aerial relating to the air aerospace air and space
ambul	walk	amble to walk in a slow, relaxed way ambulant walking or moving around ambulatory able to walk
ami amo	love	amiable friendly, pleasant, lovable amity friendly and peaceful relations amorous showing romantic love
anim	life, spirit	animal a living organism animate to make alive inanimate not alive or active
ann enn	year	anniversary a date observed once a year annual happening once a year millennium 1,000 years

Roots	Root Meanings	Sample Words and Definitions
arch	chief	architect a person who designs buildings matriarch a female who rules a group monarch a king or queen
archa archae archi	primitive, ancient	archaeology the scientific study of ancient cultures archaic belonging to an earlier period archive a collection of historical materials
art	skill	artifact object made by a person's skill artisan a person skilled in a craft artist a person who creates something with skill
audi	hear	audible loud enough to be heard audience people who see and hear a program audiovisual relating to sound and vision
belli	war	antebellum before a war bellicose ready to fight belligerent hostile, ready to fight
cardi	heart	cardiac relating to the heart cardiogenic resulting from a disease of the heart cardiologist a heart doctor
cede ceed	go, yield	exceed to go beyond the limits proceed to go before someone recede to go back
ceive cept	take	accept to take a thing that is offered perceive to take notice of something receive to take or accept something given

Roots	Root Meanings	Sample Words and Definitions
cert	sure	ascertain to find out something with certainty certain being absolutely sure certify to state that something is true
chron	time	chronic lasting for a long time chronological arrangement of events in time order synchronize happen at the same time
cide cise	cut, kill	homicide murder incisor a sharp tooth for cutting food insecticide a chemical used to kill insects
claim clam	shout, speak out	clamor to shout and make noise exclaim to cry out loudly and suddenly proclaim to announce something publicly
clar	clear	clarification an explanation clarify to make something clear declare to state something clearly
cline	lean	inclination a feeling or leaning toward incline a surface that slopes or leans recline to lean back and relax
clud	shut	exclude to shut out include to make part of the group; to not shut out seclude to shut off from others
cogn	know	cognizant having knowledge incognito disguised so no one knows you recognize to know a thing, person, etc.

Roots	Root Meanings	Sample Words and Definitions
commun	common	communal owned by everyone in common commune a group that shares everything community people who live in a common area
corp	body	corporation a company recognized by law as a single body corpse a dead body
cosm	universe	cosmonaut a Russian astronaut cosmos the universe microcosm a miniature universe
cracy crat	rule	aristocrat a member of the ruling class bureaucrat an official who applies rules rigidly theocracy government ruled by a god or priests
cred	believe	credence belief that something is true or valid credulous believing things too easily; gullible incredible unbelievable
cycl	circle, ring	bicycle a vehicle with two wheels cycle a sequence that is repeated cyclone a storm with circling winds
dent	tooth	dental relating to teeth dentist a doctor trained to treat teeth dentures a set of false teeth
dict	speak	contradict to speak against someone's statement diction clarity of speaking predict say in advance what is going to happen

Roots	Root Meanings	Sample Words and Definitions
domin	master	dominate to be the master of domineering excessively controlling predominate to have more power than others
don donat	give	donation a contribution or gift donor someone who gives something pardon to give forgiveness for an offense
duc duct	lead	conduct to lead musicians in playing music deduct to subtract, to lead away educate to lead to knowledge
fac	make, do	artifact an object made by a person factory a place where things are made malefactor a person who does wrong
fer	bear, bring, carry	confer to bring an honor to someone ferry a boat that carries passengers transfer to move to another place
flect	bend	deflect to bend course because of hitting something inflection a bending in the voice's tone or pitch
fract frag	break	fracture a break in a bone fragile easy to break fragment a small piece broken off
fug	flee, run away, escape	fugitive a person who is running away refuge a sheltered place to flee to refugee a person seeking protection

Roots	Root Meanings	Sample Words and Definitions
funct	perform, work	defunct no longer working or alive function to work or perform a role normally malfunction to fail to work correctly
gen	birth, race	genealogy the study of the history of a family generation all the people born at approximately the same time
gon	angle	decagon a polygon with 10 angles diagonal a slanting line (on an angle) octagon a geometrical figure with 8 angles
gram	letter, written	diagram a simple drawing grammar rules of how to write words in sentences telegram a message sent by telegraph
graph	write	autograph a person's handwritten signature stenography writing in shorthand telegraph long-distance writing by electrical codes
grat	pleasing	gratify to please someone gratitude feeling of thanks for something pleasant ingrate a person who doesn't say thanks
iatr	medical care	geriatrics medical care of the elderly pediatrician a doctor who treats children podiatry a branch of medicine that cares for feet
imag	likeness	image a likeness of someone imaginative able to think up new ideas or images imagine to form a picture or likeness in the mind

Roots	Root Meanings	Sample Words and Definitions
ject	throw	eject to throw someone out interject to throw a remark into a discussion project to cast or throw something
jud	law	judgment a decision of a court of law judicial having to do with judges or courts of law judiciary a system of courts of law
junct	join	conjunction a word that joins parts of sentences disjunction a disconnection junction a place where two things join
lab	work	collaborate to work with a person elaborate to work out the details laborious requiring a lot of hard work
liber	free	liberate to set free libertine a person with a free, wild lifestyle liberty freedom
loc	place	dislocate to put something out of its usual place locale a place relocate to move to a new place
luc	light	elucidate to explain; to throw light on lucid easily understood; giving off light translucent allowing light through
luna	moon	lunar relating to the moon lunarscape the surface of the moon lunatic insane (as if driven mad by the moon)

Roots	Root Meanings	Sample Words and Definitions
man	hand	maneuver to move with the hand manual done with the hands manuscript a book written by hand
mand	to order	command an order or instruction demand a hard-to-ignore order mandate an official order
mania	madness, insanity	bibliomania a crazy love of books egomania a mad love of oneself maniac an insane person
mar	sea	marina a harbor for pleasure boats maritime relating to the sea submarine an undersea boat
mater matri	mother	maternal relating to motherhood maternity the state of being a mother matriarch a woman head of a household
max	greatest	maximal the best or greatest possible maximize to make as great as possible maximum the greatest amount
merge mers	dip, dive	immerge to put or dip something into a liquid immerse to put or dip something into a liquid submerge to dip something into water
meter	measure	audiometer an instrument that measures hearing chronometer an instrument that measures time gravimeter an instrument that measures gravity

Roots	Root Meanings	Sample Words and Definitions
migr	move	immigrant a person who moves to a new country to settle migrant person who moves from place to place
min	small, less	mini something that is very small minuscule extremely tiny minutiae very small or trivial details
miss	send	dismiss to send someone away missile a weapon sent into the air transmission something sent by satellite, wire, radio waves, etc.
mit	send	emit to send something out remit to send payment to someone submit to send something in for consideration
mob	move	immobilize to stop from moving mobile able to move freely snowmobile a vehicle that moves over snow
mort	death	immortal living forever; unable to die mortal certain to die mortician an undertaker
mot	move	motion the act of moving motivate to move someone to action promote to move someone forward
mov	move	immovable fixed, not movable movie rapidly projected pictures that "move" remove to move away from a place

Roots	Root Meanings	Sample Words and Definitions
mut	change	immutable **not changing** mutant **an organism that has undergone a change** mutate **to undergo a change**
narr	tell	narrate **to tell a story** narrative **a story** narrator **a person who tells a story**
nat	born	innate **inborn, native, natural** natal **relating to birth** natural **gotten at birth, not afterward**
nav	ship	circumnavigate **to sail around a place** naval **relating to a navy or warships** navigate **to sail a ship through a place**
neg	no	negate **to say, "No, it didn't happen."** negative **meaning "no"** renege **to go back on a promise**
not	mark	notable **worthy of being marked for attention** notarize **to certify a signature on a legal document by affixing an official stamp or mark**
noun nunc	declare	announce **to declare in public** denounce **to declare harsh criticism** enunciate **to speak or declare something clearly**
nov	new	innovate **to introduce a new way** novelty **something new** novice **a person who is new at a job**

Roots	Root Meanings	Sample Words and Definitions
numer	number	enumerate to name a number of items on a list numerology the study of magical uses of numbers numerous a large number
ocu	eye	binoculars 2-lens device for seeing distances monocular relating to one eye oculist an eye doctor
opt	eye	optic relating to the eyes optical relating to sight optician a person who fits eyeglasses
opt	best	optimal the best, the most desirable optimize to make the best of optimum the best something could be
pater	father	paternal relating to fathers paternity fatherhood patriarch a man who rules a group
path	feeling, emotion	antipathy a feeling of great anger apathy a lack of feeling or interest empathy ability to understand another's feelings
pel	drive, force	compel to force someone to act expel to drive someone out of a place repel to force back
phon	sound	cacophony loud, unpleasant sounds microphone a device that makes sounds louder phonetic relating to human speech sounds

Roots	Root Meanings	Sample Words and Definitions
photo	light	photogenic caused by light photograph image made on light-sensitive film photon the smallest possible unit of light
phys	nature, medicine, the body	physical relating to the body physician a doctor physique nature, shape, and size of one's body
pod	foot	podiatrist a foot doctor podium a small platform to stand on tripod a stand or frame with 3 legs
poli	city	metropolis a large city police people who work for the government to maintain order in a city politics actions of a government or political party
pon	place, put	opponent a person who places him/herself against an action, idea, etc. postpone to put off doing something
pop	people	popular appealing to a lot of people population all of the people who live in a place populist a supporter of the rights of people
port	carry	export to carry goods out of a place portable able to be carried porter a person who carries luggage
pos	place	deposit to place or drop something expose to place out in the open for all to see position the place where someone is

Roots	Root Meanings	Sample Words and Definitions
psych	mind, soul	psyche the human spirit or soul psychic relating to the human mind psychology the study of the mind
pul	urge	compulsion a very strong urge expulsion the urging out of someone impulsive having an urge to do something
put	think	computer an electronic thinking device dispute to disagree with what another person thinks
reg	guide, rule	regent a person who rules on behalf of a king or queen regime a government that rules
rid	laugh	deride to make fun of someone ridicule to make fun or mock ridiculous silly, causing laughter
rupt	break	bankrupt unable to pay because you're "broke" interrupt to break in, to disturb rupture a break in something
san	health	sane mentally healthy sanitary relating to cleanliness and health sanitation maintenance of public health
scend	climb, go	ascend to climb upward crescendo a climbing up of the volume of music descend to go or climb down

Roots	Root Meanings	Sample Words and Definitions
sci	know	conscience sense of knowing right from wrong conscious knowing what is happening omniscient knowing everything
scope	see	microscope a device used to see tiny things periscope a seeing instrument on a submarine telescope a device used to see distances
scribe script	write	inscribe to write letters or words on a surface scribe a person who writes out documents transcribe to write an exact copy of something
serv	save, keep	conserve to save or keep something safe preserve to save something reservation a place kept for a person
sol	alone	desolate lonely, dismal, gloomy solitary done alone, by yourself solo a performance done by one person alone
son	sound	consonant a speech sound sonorous producing loud, full, rich sounds supersonic faster than sound
soph	wise	philosopher a wise person who explains about life sophist a person who is wise in dishonest debating sophisticated wise about the ways of the world
spec	see, look	circumspect cautious, looking all around retrospective a looking back at past things spectator a person who sees an event

Roots	Root Meanings	Sample Words and Definitions
sphere	ball	biosphere the whole round surface of the earth hemisphere half the earth spherical shaped like a ball
sta	stand	stable standing steady and firm stagnant standing still, not moving stationary at a standstill, fixed
stell	star	constellation a group of stars that forms a pattern interstellar between the stars stellar relating to stars
struct	build	construct to build destruction the act of destroying something that was built structure something built
sum	highest	sum the combined total of everything; the limit summation the total, highest amount summit the highest point or top
tact tang	touch	contact a state in which two things touch tactile relating to the sense of touch tangible able to be touched
temp	time	contemporary existing at the same time temporal relating to time temporary lasting for a limited time
term	end	determine to find something out at the end of an investigation terminate to end

Roots	Root Meanings	Sample Words and Definitions
terr	land, earth	extraterrestrial existing outside the earth terrain ground or land territory an area of land
the theo	god	monotheism belief in one god polytheism worshiping more than one god theology the study of religion, god, etc.
therm	heat	thermal relating to heat thermos an insulated jar that keeps heat in or out thermostat a device that controls heat
tox	poison	detoxification the process of removing poisons toxic poisonous toxicology the study of poisons
tract	pull, drag	attract to pull objects nearer distract to drag attention away from something tractor a motor vehicle that pulls things
urb	city	suburb residential area on the edge of a city urban relating to a city urbanology the study of city life
vac	empty	evacuate to empty a dangerous place vacant empty, not occupied vacation a time empty of work
ver	truth	veracious truthful, honest veracity the truth verify to prove that something is true

Roots	Root Meanings	Sample Words and Definitions
vict vinc	conquer	convince to win someone over invincible not able to be conquered victory the conquest of an enemy
vid vis	see	evident clearly seen vision the ability to see vista a big, wide view
voc vok	voice	advocate to speak in favor of vocal relating to the voice vocalize to produce with your voice
vol	wish, will	benevolent showing good will and kindness malevolent showing bad will voluntary resulting from your own free will
vor	eat	herbivorous eating plants omnivorous eating plants and animals savory delicious, flavorful

SUFFIXES

> **Suffix:** the part added to the end of the word after the root. It can often add information to the root or change the meaning or part of speech of the word.

Here are some of the most popular suffixes in English, along with a bunch of words that have those suffixes.

Note: The hyphen (-) in front of the suffix shows that it is not a whole word, only the end of it, and that part of the word comes before it.

Suffix	Suffix Meanings	Sample Words and Definitions
-able	able to be	excitable **able to be easily excited** portable **able to be carried** preventable **able to be prevented**
-ade	act, action, or process; product	blockade **an action to block people or goods** cavalcade **a procession of cars, carriages, etc.** promenade **action of leisurely strolling in public**
-age	action or process	passage **the act of going place to place** pilgrimage **a journey to a holy place** voyage **a journey to a distant place**
-al	relating to	bacterial **relating to bacteria** natural **relating to nature** theatrical **relating to the theater**
-an -ian	relating to, belonging to	American **of or relating to America** Italian **of or relating to Italy** urban **of or relating to a city**
-ance	state or quality of	annoyance **the state of being annoyed** brilliance **the quality of being brilliant** defiance **the act of defying; bold resistance**
-ant	a person who	applicant **a person who applies for something** immigrant **a person who settles in a new country** servant **a person who serves**

Suffix	Suffix Meanings	Sample Words and Definitions
-ant	inclined to, tending to	brilliant inclined to be extremely bright defiant tending to disobey vigilant inclined to be alert to danger
-ar	of or relating to; being	lunar relating to a moon molecular relating to molecules solar relating to the sun
-ar	a person who	beggar a person who begs burglar a person who enters a place to steal liar one who tells lies
-ard	a person who does an action	coward a person who is easily frightened sluggard a person who avoids work wizard a person who is very skilled at something
-arian	a person who	disciplinarian a person who enforces all rules vegetarian a person who eats vegetables, not meat and fish
-ary	of or relating to	budgetary relating to budgets literary relating to literature military relating to armed forces
-ate	state or quality of	affectionate the quality of showing affection desolate the state of being deserted, uninhabited obstinate the quality of being stubborn, inflexible
-ate	makes the word a verb	activate to make something active evaporate to change liquid into vapor medicate to give medicine to

Suffix	Suffix Meanings	Sample Words and Definitions
-ation	action or process	creation the act of causing something to exist emancipation the act of setting free narration the process of telling a story
-ative	tending to (makes the word an adjective)	creative inclined to create things preservative inclined to protect from spoiling talkative inclined to talk a lot
-cy	state, condition, or quality	belligerency the state of being at war efficiency quality of being efficient and capable privacy condition of being private and secluded
-dom	condition of, quality of	boredom the state of being bored freedom the state of living and acting freely stardom the condition of being a star
-ed -d	past tense	called did call hammered did hammer laughed did laugh
-en	makes the word a verb	awaken to wake up fasten to attach something firmly strengthen to make stronger
-ence	state or condition; action	absence the state of being away dependence the action of depending negligence the condition of being careless
-ent	inclined to	competent inclined to be able to do a job different inclined to not be the same as potent inclined to be extremely powerful

Suffix	Suffix Meanings	Sample Words and Definitions
-er	more	bigger more big faster more fast happier more happy
-er	action or process	fluster to make someone nervous ponder to think carefully stutter to say something haltingly
-er	a person who	announcer a person who announces barber a person who cuts hair teacher a person who teaches
-ern	state or quality of	eastern the state of being east of a place northern the state of being north of a place western the state of being west of a place
-ery -ry -y	trade, job, activity	archery the activity of shooting arrows with a bow dentistry the job of caring for people's teeth robbery the act of stealing from somebody
-ese	relating to a place	Chinese relating to China Congolese relating to the Congo Japanese relating to Japan
-ess	female	actress a female actor heiress a female heir lioness a female lion (see pages 164–165, Avoiding Sexist Language)
-est	most	funniest the most funny hottest the most hot silliest the most silly

Suffix	Suffix Meanings	Sample Words and Definitions
-etic	relating to (makes the word an adjective)	athletic relating to athletes energetic relating to energy poetic relating to poetry
-ful	full of	cheerful full of cheer helpful full of help thankful full of thanks
-fy	makes the word a verb	amplify to make larger or louder falsify to state untruthfully terrify to frighten someone a lot
-hood	state, condition, or quality	childhood the state of being a child motherhood the state of being a mother sainthood the condition of being a saint
-ible	able to be	audible able to be heard legible able to be read plausible able to be believed
-ic -ical	relating to, characterized by	analytical relating to analysis comic relating to or marked by comedy organic characteristic of living things
-ile	relating to, capable of	agile capable of moving quickly with skill docile capable of being quiet and easily taught volatile capable of becoming violent
-ily	in what manner	sloppily in a sloppy manner steadily in a steady manner zanily in a zany, weird manner

Suffix	Suffix Meanings	Sample Words and Definitions
-ine	relating to	canine relating to dogs feminine relating to women and girls masculine relating to men and boys
-ing	action or process	dancing the action of taking part in a dance seeing the action of looking at something writing the process of putting words on paper
-ing	materials	bedding materials to cover a bed frosting materials to cover a cake with icing roofing materials used to make a roof
-ion	action or process	celebration the act of celebrating completion the act of completing navigation the process of sailing
-ious	having the qualities of; full of	ambitious full of ambition cautious full of caution gracious having qualities of kindness and grace
-ish	relating to, character-istic of	apish resembling an ape brutish cruel and ruthless like a brute childish like a child; immature, silly
-ism	state or quality; principles	altruism quality of unselfish concern for others despotism the process of rule by a despot heroism the condition of being a hero
-ist	one who does an action	artist a person who creates art linguist a person who speaks languages pianist a person who plays the piano

Suffix	Suffix Meanings	Sample Words and Definitions
-ity	state, condition, or quality	abnormality the condition of not being normal civility the quality of politeness necessity the condition of being necessary
-ive	inclined to	attractive inclined to attract expensive tending to cost a lot of money repulsive tending to repel or drive back
-ization	act or process of making	colonization the process of establishing a colony fertilization the act of fertilizing modernization the process of making more modern
-ize	to cause to become	antagonize to cause a person to become angry authorize to give someone power or authority popularize to make something widely liked
-less	without	fearless without fear helpless without power or strength; weak homeless without a home
-like	resembling, character-istic of	childlike characteristic of a child homelike like home lifelike resembling real life
-ly	in what manner (makes an adverb)	badly in a bad, inferior manner courageously in a courageous, brave manner quickly in a quick, speedy manner
-ment	act or process	movement the act of moving or changing place placement the act of placing or arranging shipment the process of shipping something

Suffix	Suffix Meanings	Sample Words and Definitions
-ness	state or quality (makes a noun)	kindness the state of being kind shyness the condition of being shy weakness the condition of being weak
-ology	study of, science of	anthropology the study of humankind archaeology the study of past cultures biology the study of all forms of life
-or	a person who	inventor a person who invents legislator a person who makes laws translator a person who translates
-ory	place for	armory an arsenal where weapons are stored dormitory a college building where people sleep laboratory a place where scientific work is done
-ous	full of	hazardous full of dangers humorous full of humor wondrous full of wonders
-phobia	abnormal fear of	acrophobia fear of high places claustrophobia fear of confined spaces xenophobia fear of foreign people
-ship	state or condition of; skill of	authorship the skill of being an author citizenship the condition of being a citizen friendship the state of being a friend
-sion	state or quality	confusion the state of being confused depression the state of hopelessness tension the state of being anxious, nervous, edgy

Suffix	Suffix Meanings	Sample Words and Definitions
-some	character-ized by or tending to	awesome tending to cause awe or amazement bothersome inclined to bother or irritate lonesome inclined to be lonely or friendless
-th	state or quality	depth the quality of being deep length the state of being long strength the quality of being strong
-tion	state or quality	attention the state of mentally focusing caution the state of taking care to avoid risk fascination the state of being very interested
-tude	state, condition, or quality	fortitude the quality of having strength and endurance gratitude the state of feeling grateful
-ty	state, condition, or quality	ability the state of being able to do something honesty the condition of being honest and open loyalty the quality of being loyal and faithful
-ular	relating to or resembling	cellular relating to living cells circular resembling a circle muscular relating to muscles
-uous	state or quality of	arduous the state of requiring hard work tumultuous quality of being noisy and rowdy virtuous quality of having moral goodness
-ure	action, condition, or process	closure the action of ending erasure the action of erasing failure the action of failing

Suffix	Suffix Meanings	Sample Words and Definitions
-ward	shows specified direction	backward **in the opposite direction** eastward **toward the east** homeward **in the direction of home**
-wise	in what manner or direction	clockwise **in the direction that clock hands move** lengthwise **in the direction of the length** otherwise **in another manner or way**
-y	made up of, character-ized by	brainy **characterized by intelligence** fruity **consisting of or like fruit** gooey **made up of goo**

EXTRA

We learned in this chapter that prefixes change the meanings of the words they're attached to. Well, this is the story of one prefix that doesn't, and that's caused a lot of confusion over the years.

If you saw a big gasoline truck driving by with the words DANGER FLAMMABLE in fiery red letters on the side, you wouldn't be surprised. You know that gasoline can easily catch fire and burn rapidly (which is a perfect dictionary definition of flammable).

But wait a minute. Here comes another gasoline truck, and on its side are the words DANGER INFLAMMABLE. What's going on? We know that the prefix *in* means "not," so is this truck filled with gasoline that can't catch fire? There's no such thing. And if there were, why does it still say DANGER?

The amazing fact is that both the words FLAMMABLE and INFLAMMABLE mean exactly the same thing: able to catch fire easily and burn rapidly. Look them up in your dictionary and see for yourself.

They both come from Latin words: flammable from *flammare*, the verb "to set fire to," and inflammable from *inflammare*, the verb "to inflame." For years people have mistakenly thought that inflammable meant "not flammable," instead of just the opposite. But you'll never get them mixed up because now you know the truth.

If you want to warn people about something that can easily be set aflame, put up a sign that says DANGER FLAMMABLE and forget about INFLAMMABLE, so that nobody will get the wrong idea.

chapter 3

Tricky Words

Sound-Alikes, Spell-Alikes, and Look-Alikes

Homonyms

What does this sentence mean?

A buoy eye no eight a peace of bred and jamb.

If you read that sentence out loud to a hundred people, nobody would hear a mistake. If you typed it on your computer and spellchecked it, your spellchecker would say it was perfect. There's nothing wrong with the spelling of any of the words in the sentence, but seven of the words are wrong. How can that be?

All of the mistakes are words that sound the same as the correct words but are spelled differently and have different meanings. Teachers sometimes call these pairs of words *homonyms* or *homophones*. Your spellchecker cannot spot words that are not spelled wrong.

Here's the same sentence with all the correct words:

A boy I know ate a piece of bread and jam.

There are hundreds of pairs (and sometimes trios) of these tricky homonyms. If you know how to tell them apart, you will know how to put the right vocabulary word in the right place. Here are some of the most common homonyms, in sentences that will help you get them straight.

If you **add** *(combine numbers to get a sum)* up the prices in this **ad** *(advertisement)*, you'll see what this car really costs.

He will **ail** *(feel ill)* if he drinks all that **ale** *(liquor)*.

Some fresh **air** *(mixture of nitrogen and oxygen)* blew onto the face of the **heir** *(person who inherits)* to the throne.

Walk down the **aisle** *(passageway between seats)* on the **isle** *(small island)* with me, and **I'll** *(I will)* marry you.

When I saw him at the **altar** *(ceremonial church table)*, I said that someone should **alter** *(adjust and change)* his new suit.

A tiny **ant** *(insect)* was crawling up the leg of my **aunt** *(uncle's wife)*.

He got sick because he **ate** *(devoured)* at least **eight** *(number between seven and nine)* hot dogs at the ball game.

The totally **bald** *(hairless)* man really **bawled** *(cried out loud)* when his toupee blew off.

That **bare** *(naked)* animal in the picture is a grizzly **bear** *(furry animal)* without fur.

The fields of the **baron** *(nobleman)* were always **barren** *(not able to grow crops)*, so he built houses on the land.

She put flowers at the **base** *(bottom)* of the statue of the famous **bass** *(low in pitch, deep in tone)* singer.

At the edge of the **beach** *(seashore)* was a tall **beech** *(tree with smooth gray bark)*.

The cafeteria lady won't really **beat** *(hit)* you if you don't eat this **beet** *(dark-red root vegetable)*, will she?

My sister's **beau** *(boyfriend)* gave her a beautiful **bow** *(ribbon tied in loops)* for her hair.

Can a **bee** *(insect)* that can sting you really **be** *(exist as)* a good pet?

The art teacher has **been** *(past of be)* searching in the crayon **bin** *(storage box)* for just the right shade of red.

Behind the berry *(small, juicy fruit)* bush, the dog will bury *(hide in the ground)* its favorite bone.

In the upper berth *(built-in bed)* of the train, the passengers witnessed the birth *(being born)* of the kittens.

He was billed *(charged)* a lot of money for the land on which he wanted to build *(construct)* a factory.

He blew *(did blow)* his nose into the blue *(color)* handkerchief.

Do you think the wild boar *(male pig)* will bore *(make a hole)* through the fence and escape?

When the carpenter kept talking about his favorite board *(piece of wood)*, I got very bored *(tired of listening)*.

The athlete was bold *(brave)* when he bowled *(rolled bowling balls)* against the world champion

The landlady searched along the border *(line that separates places)* for her missing boarder *(person who rents a room)*.

In this borough *(part of a city)*, ride around on your burro *(small donkey)*, and you'll find a rabbit burrow *(hole)*.

The bow *(front section)* of this ship was made from the bough *(large branch)* of a mighty oak.

Boy *(male child)*, make sure that you don't sail near that buoy *(floating warning signal)* in the water.

The brake *(stopping device)* on your bike will break *(split into pieces)* if you press it too hard.

The way she buttered her bread *(baked food)* showed you that she was very well bred *(brought up)*.

The bridal *(wedding)* party rode along the bridle *(track for riding horses)* path to the wedding.

She needed an eyebrow pencil for her brows *(lines of hair over the eyes)*, so she went to browse *(look)* in a drugstore.

You may play with your friend, but *(however)* don't butt *(hit)* your heads against each other.

If you go by *(near)* the mall, could you please buy *(purchase)* a few things for me?

In the capital *(main, chief)* city, we must visit the capitol *(building where the legislature meets)*.

The king's pet rabbit held a carrot *(orange vegetable)* made of 14-carat (also spelled karat—*unit of measure of gold*) gold.

There's a crack in the ceiling *(top of room)*, so I'm sealing *(filling)* it with plaster.

In the prison cell *(small room)*, the prisoner was making dolls to sell *(give up for money)* when he got out.

In the cellar *(room under a house)*, the seller *(person who sells)* of the house showed me his wood-paneled basement.

For just a cent *(penny)*, this perfume will be sent *(dispatched)* to your girlfriend, who will like the scent *(smell)*.

Even though this pet canary is cheap *(not expensive)*, its cheep *(chirping sound)* is loud.

After she chews *(grinds with her teeth)* this stick of gum for an hour, she will choose *(select)* another flavor.

How can you play this chord *(musical sound)* on your guitar with this cord *(string)* tied around your fingers?

Can you **cite** *(quote)* a passage from Shakespeare about this lovely **site** *(place, location)* within our **sight** *(vision, view)*?

There's a **clause** *(section)* in the lion tamer's contract that says that the lions' **claws** *(nails)* must be clipped every day.

Please **close** *(shut)* the door to the **clothes** *(wearing apparel, garments)* closet before moths get in.

At the **coal** *(black mineral used as fuel)* miners' picnic, they served plenty of **cole**slaw *(shredded cabbage)*.

A **coarse** *(rude, bad-mannered)* person doesn't make many friends in the **course** *(progress, path, duration)* of life.

The army **colonel** *(officer)* almost choked on a hard **kernel** *(seed in a nut)* of unpopped popcorn.

This dessert will **complement** *(perfectly complete)* the dinner, and everyone will **compliment** *(praise)* my cooking.

The city **council** *(group of people)* held an important meeting to offer **counsel** *(advice and guidance)* to those in need.

I heard the **creak** *(squeaky, harsh noise)* of the dock just before it collapsed into the raging **creek** *(stream)*.

Of all the **crews** *(groups of workers)* I've known, this **cruise** *(pleasure voyage)* ship has the best people.

This golden **cymbal** *(clashing brass musical instrument)* is a **symbol** *(sign, representation)* of the royal orchestra.

That large **cypress** *(evergreen tree)* comes from **Cyprus** *(an island country in the eastern Mediterranean Sea)*.

During his first few **days** *(periods of 24 hours)* in high school, he was in a **daze** *(confused or bewildered condition)*.

Look out the window, **dear** *(beloved, darling)*, and you'll see a beautiful **deer** *(animal)* on our lawn.

The guard won't **desert** *(abandon)* his post until after he eats his favorite **dessert** *(food served at the end of a meal)*.

By morning's **dew** *(moisture on the ground)*, I will **do** *(accomplish)* all I can to repay the debt that is **due** *(owed)*.

She will **die** *(stop living, expire)* laughing when she finds out that you want to **dye** *(color)* your hair purple and green.

My pet **doe** *(female deer)* loves to eat a pastry made of sugar and **dough** *(a mixture of flour and water)*.

Many **does** *(female deer)* love to **doze** *(sleep)* in a cool, shady forest on a hot, sunny day.

Two pairs of people will fight with swords, so we'll see a **dual** *(made of two parts)* **duel** *(fight between two persons)*.

How much can a potter **earn** *(get paid)* for making copies of this ancient Greek **urn** *(vase)*?

A **ewe** *(female sheep)* likes the shade under a **yew** *(poisonous evergreen tree)*, **you** *(person spoken to)* know.

Something flew into my left **eye** *(organ of vision)* and **I** *(myself)* couldn't see clearly.

I don't think it's **fair** *(proper, right, just)* that this airline charges full **fare** *(price for traveling)* for a baby.

It was quite a **feat** *(accomplishment, deed)* for the elf to win this race with his tiny **feet** *(lower parts of legs)*.

I must **find** *(locate)* the judge who **fined** *(charged money as a punishment)* me so that I can pay her what I owe.

On the bark of the **fir** *(evergreen)* tree we found traces of the animal's **fur** *(thick coat of soft fur)*.

The little **flea** *(insect)* tried to **flee** *(run away)* when it heard the dog's loud bark.

The bird **flew** *(did fly)* down the **flue** *(pipe inside a chimney)* when it caught the **flu** *(influenza, contagious viral infection)*.

From dough made of water and **flour** *(ground grain)*, she made a cake shaped like a **flower** *(plant with blossoms)*.

For *(over time)* at least **four** *(number after three)* years I've shouted, "**Fore!**" *("Watch out!")* before I hit the golf ball.

At the signal from the principal, you should bring **forth** *(forward)* the **fourth** *(number after third)* grade.

If the chicken plays in the dirt, it's a **foul** *(dirty)* **fowl** *(a bird like a duck, goose, turkey, or chicken)*.

The artist will **freeze** *(become cold and icy)* while painting the **frieze** *(horizontal picture at the top of a wall)* unless the king **frees** *(discharges)* him from this frigid task.

He had a very peculiar **gait** *(way of walking)* as he opened the **gate** *(door in a fence)* and entered the secret garden.

He had to learn to **gild** *(cover with gold)* picture frames before he could get into the framers' **guild** *(workers' group)*.

Her fingerprints on the **gilt** *(coating of gold)* were proof of her **guilt** *(deserving of blame)*.

The old **gnu** *(African antelope)* at the zoo was replaced by a **new** *(different)* gnu, but you **knew** *(were aware of)* that.

This antique fireplace **grate** *(a framework of metal bars used to hold fuel)* would look **great** *(terrific)* in my new house.

In **Greece** *(a country of southeastern Europe)*, people don't usually cook with so much **grease** *(thick, oily substance, fat)*.

This **grisly** *(horrible, awful)* picture shows what the teeth and claws of a **grizzly** *(large brown or gray bear)* bear can do.

My brother will **groan** *(moan)* when he sees how his list of chores has **grown** *(increased in size)*.

Nobody would have **guessed** *(supposed, thought)* that the necklace was stolen by a **guest** *(invited visitor)* at the party.

Even in sleet and **hail** *(ice pellets that fall from the sky)*, my grandfather is a **hale** *(healthy, vigorous)* and hearty soul.

In the banquet **hall** *(large room)* the waiters had to **haul** *(pull, drag)* the tables from one end of the room to the other.

When the pilot reached the **hangar** *(a building for planes)*, he hung his jacket on a **hanger** *(device for hanging clothes)*.

When the cyclone hit the **hare** *(animal like a rabbit)*, it blew away all its **hair** *(fur)*.

When he started to throw **hay** *(dried grass)* on my head, I shouted, "**Hey,** *(word used to attract attention)* stop that!"

He is asking the foot doctor to **heal** *(cure)* his sore **heel** *(back part of the foot)*, or **he'll** *(he will)* be in great pain.

Alexander Graham Bell told his assistant, "Put your ear to the telephone tube and **hear** *(listen)* **here** *(in this place)*."

The cattle were happy when they **heard** *(did hear)* what the cowboy had said about their **herd** *(group of cows)*.

Before you can go **higher** *(up and up)* in this company, you have to get them to **hire** *(employ, give a job to)* you.

Just listen to **him** *(that man)* sing that beautiful **hymn** *(sacred song of praise or joy)*.

The trainer shouted herself **hoarse** *(having a rough voice)* trying to teach the **horse** *(large hoofed mammal)* new tricks.

This big general store sells everything from **hoes** *(weeding tools)* to **hose** *(socks)*.

The dog dug a **hole** *(opening in the ground)* in the backyard and buried his **whole** *(total, complete)* supply of bones in it.

People in this **holy** *(sacred)* place are **wholly** *(totally, completely)* devoted to doing good deeds.

Every **hour** *(60 minutes)*, when the clock chimes, **our** *(belongs to us)* dog starts to howl loudly.

The sky turned a golden **hue** *(shade of color)* as **Hugh** *(man's name)* started to **hew** *(cut)* down trees.

The once famous rock-and-roll **idol** *(adored person)* has recently been very **idle** *(out of work, not busy)*.

She found the secret treasure map behind the oak bookcase **in** *(inside)* the old **inn** *(country hotel)*.

He didn't wash his hands after lunch and got peanut butter and **jam** *(jelly)* on the newly painted door **jamb** *(side of door)*.

The captain lost the **key** *(device that opens a lock)* to the **quay** *(wharf)* and couldn't get back onto his boat.

Sir Pitch of Dark, a famous **knight** *(Medieval soldier)* in shining armor, fought dragons only at **night** *(after sunset)*.

How can the mother louse **knit** *(loop yarn together)* her child a sweater when it's still only a **nit** *(insect egg)*?

The **knot** *(tied rope)* was so tightly tied that even the experienced sailor was **not** *(in no way)* able to loosen it.

If she asks if you **know** *(have information about)* who broke the window, just say, "**No** *(opposite of yes)*."

Who **knows** *(has knowledge of)* the shape of an aardvark's **nose** *(organ of smell)*?

Because he was tired from walking along that long **lane** *(country road)*, he has **lain** *(rested his body)* down to sleep.

There was a **leak** *(crack, hole)* in my bowl, and my potato-and-**leek** *(edible plant like an onion)* soup dripped out.

She **leased** *(rented)* an apartment for the **least** *(smallest)* amount of money.

The guide **led** *(showed people the way)* us on a tour through the abandoned **lead** *(soft, gray metal)* mine.

If you finish the **lesson** *(something to be learned)* in class, the teacher will **lessen** *(reduce)* your homework assignment.

She called him a **liar** *(person who lies)* when he said he didn't break her **lyre** *(stringed instrument like a harp)*.

Don't **lie** *(give a false answer)* when he asks you what you did with the **lye** *(strong substance used to make soap)*.

After the **lightning** *(flash of electric discharge in the air)* struck, the dark sky started **lightening** *(becoming brighter)*.

The zoologist drew links *(links)* between these particular lynx *(wildcats)* and other kinds of wildcats of North America.

We were happy to loan *(lend)* an umbrella to the lone *(single, solitary)* hiker.

The bed was made *(done)* perfectly by the new maid *(woman servant)*.

The main *(most important)* thing is to cut off that mane *(a long, thick growth of hair)* when you visit your grandparents in Maine *(state in the northeast United States)*.

To find the field of maize *(yellow/orange corn)*, you must get out of this maze *(confusing pathways)* of bushes.

A male *(masculine)* postal carrier used to deliver our mail *(letters)*, but now we have a female mail deliverer.

In what manner *(way)* will you redecorate this beautiful country manor *(the main house on an estate, a mansion)*?

On the brass hook next to the mantel *(shelf over a fireplace)* he hung his new woolen mantle *(cloak)*.

Your sister will maul *(beat)* you if you lose all the stuff she bought at the mall *(shopping center)*.

The old butcher told the new butcher, "There's some meat *(edible flesh)* I'd like you to meet *(be introduced to)*."

If you meddle *(interfere)* in other people's business, don't expect to be given a medal *(award)* for curiosity.

For displaying mettle *(courage)* in battle, he won a badge of gold-colored metal *(hard, shiny chemical substance)*.

You can **mince** *(cut into small pieces)* this meat, but leave all those chocolate **mints** *(flavored candies)* in the kitchen alone.

A person can't be hired as a coal **miner** *(person who digs out ore)* if he or she is still a **minor** *(under legal age)*.

Do you think a tiny **mite** *(an insect like a spider)* has a lot of **might** *(strength)*?

Your dad will **moan** *(make a sad sound)* when he finds out that the lawn has not been **mown** *(cut down)*.

This **morning** *(dawn)* the gardener is in **mourning** *(grief)* for his favorite tree, which blew down in the storm.

There was a **naval** *(having to do with ships)* scene tattooed above the sailor's **navel** *(belly button)*.

To make bread, you **need** *(have to, must)* to **knead** *(squeeze and press)* dough.

Of all the people I knew then, **none** *(not one)* was more loving than my teacher, a **nun** *(woman of a religious order)*.

Put your **oar** *(paddle)* into the water and row **o'er** *(over)* the lake toward the mine with the iron **ore** *(mineral)*, **or** *(otherwise)* we won't win the race.

This **ode** *(poem)* to nature is **owed** *(must be given)* to my poetry teacher today.

Oh *(my goodness)*, here's the quarter I **owe** *(have to pay)* you.

Two teams played in the finals, but only **one** *(number before two)* team **won** *(was the winner of)* the championship.

He **paced** *(walked)* back and forth waiting impatiently for the wallpaper **paste** *(glue)* to dry.

The president and the prime minister **packed** *(put)* a lot of details into their international trade **pact** *(treaty)*.

When she saw that all the gold dust had leaked out of the **pail** *(bucket)*, her face turned **pale** *(whitish)*.

The glazier got a sharp **pain** *(hurt, ache)* in his back trying to replace the broken window **pane** *(piece of glass)*.

Cook, please take this **pair** *(couple, two)* of knives and pare (peel) that apple and that **pear** *(fruit)*.

As he **passed** *(did pass)* by his old high school, memories of happy **past** *(from time gone by)* events flooded his mind.

A doctor has to have a lot of **patience** *(calmness)* to treat difficult **patients** *(persons who need medical care)*.

If the tiger reaches out its **paws** *(animal feet)* to you, just **pause** *(stop what you're doing)* and say, "Nice kitty."

I enjoy a lot of **peace** *(calmness)* and quiet in this little **piece** *(small part)* of the world.

At the **peak** *(top)* of the mountain, I put aside my **pique** *(anger)* and took a **peek** *(little look)* at the view.

The clown pretended he was startled by the **peal** *(loud ringing)* of the huge bell and slipped on a banana **peel** *(outer skin)*.

To make some extra money, I'm going to **pedal** *(ride a bike)* around town and **peddle** *(sell)* newspapers.

Peer *(look hard)* through these binoculars at that amazing yacht tied up at the **pier** *(wharf)*.

I'm just a **plain** *(simple, ordinary)* person who just happens to fly a jet **plane** *(flying machine)* to work every day.

On this **pole** *(long piece of wood)* I'm going to put up a sign about the **poll** *(survey of public opinion)* I'm taking.

Pore *(study carefully)* over this map, while I **pour** *(cause to flow)* you a cold drink, you **poor** *(unfortunate)* lost traveler.

I cannot **praise** *(express admiration for)* a person who **prays** *(says a prayer)* for help before he **preys** *(hunts for)* on defenseless people.

Your **presence** *(being there)* at the party is required if you are going to receive any **presents** *(gifts)* from me.

I took **pride** *(self-respect)* in minding my own business and never **pried** *(inquired closely)* into other people's lives.

If he **pries** *(forces)* open the lid of the jar, he will definitely win first **prize** *(award)* for strength.

The **principal** *(head person)* of my school is a woman of great **principle** *(high personal standards)*.

The queen will be furious when she see the **prints** *(marks)* that the **prince** *(queen's son)* made with his muddy boots.

I was sure I'd make a **profit** *(financial gain)* on this investment, but I wasn't a good **prophet** *(predictor of the future)* and lost money.

The miners dug out many **quarts** *(units that measure volume)* of **quartz** *(rock crystal)* from the sandstone and granite.

In the pouring **rain** *(water from the sky)*, during the **reign** *(time of rule)* of King Rex, I pulled on the **rein** *(narrow leather strap)* of my horse and stopped in front of the castle.

If I get a good **raise** *(increase in salary)*, I'm going to Bermuda to catch some **rays** *(beams)* of sun before they **raze** *(tear down, demolish)* my favorite hotel there.

Shh. **Rap** *(tap)* softly three times if you want me to **wrap** *(enclose)* Mom's surprise birthday present in fancy red foil.

My music teacher told me to **read** *(examine words for meaning)* the instructions on how to attach this **reed** *(flexible mouthpiece strip)* to my new clarinet.

Is it true that you caught a **real** *(actual, true)* great white shark, but that it pulled the **reel** *(spool)* right off your fishing rod?

The book with the **red** *(color)* cover is the only one that he **read** *(looked at the words of)* more than once.

The dump site needs to be covered, or it will **reek** *(smell strongly)* and **wreak** *(cause)* anger in the neighborhood.

In this fine **residence** *(home)* dwell some of the finest **residents** *(lodgers, inhabitants)* in this city.

I will have to **rest** *(relax)* a while before I can **wrest** *(pull with twisting movements)* the toy out of the hippo's mouth.

The fancy lady will probably **retch** *(throw up)* when she sees how this poor **wretch** *(unfortunate, unhappy person)* lives.

I'll show you the **right** *(correct, proper)* way to perform this **rite** *(ceremonial act)* of spring, so prepare to **write** *(put words on paper)* down the instructions.

When I **ring** *(make a ringing sound)* the bell, start to **wring** *(twist and squeeze liquid from)* out your wet towel.

Down the dusty **road** *(path)* I **rode** *(did ride)* my bike, while up the raging river she **rowed** *(paddled)* her boat.

Make sure not to disturb any roe *(fish eggs)* as you row *(paddle)* across the lake.

He got a role *(part played by a performer)* in a movie of a man in a diner munching on a roll *(round piece of bread)*.

When I arrive in Rome *(capital city of Italy)*, I plan just to roam *(wander)* all over the city seeing the sights.

Whatever she learned by rote *(memorizing by repetition)* she wrote *(did write)* down in her notebook.

My mother planted several rows *(columns, lines)* of her favorite yellow rose *(flower)*.

By the time the bell had rung *(sounded)* at the end of swim class, he had wrung *(squeezed water from)* out his swimsuit.

I can't afford a new sail *(piece of fabric to catch the wind)* for my boat until it goes on sale *(for a lower price)*.

The haunted house scene *(part or episode)* in the movie was the scariest one I had ever seen *(looked at)*.

The perfume ad said, "If you like this scent *(smell)*, it can be sent *(mailed)* to you for only a cent *(penny)*."

Does this seam *(place where two pieces of material are sewn together)* in my dress seem *(appear)* crooked?

On the high seas *(ocean)* the defeated captain sees *(watches)* the evil pirates seize *(capture)* his ship.

From the top of the lighthouse, you can really see *(observe, view)* the entire sea *(ocean)*.

After I had planted the last seed *(germ of a plant)*, I had to cede *(give up possession of)* my farm to the bank.

The **seller** *(person who sells)* of the house showed me the storage area in the **cellar** *(room under a house)*.

The **serf** *(feudal servant of a lord)* yelled, "Master, the **surf** *(waves of the sea)* is up."

I must **sew** *(stitch together)* this rip in my seed bag **so** *(in this way)* that I can **sow** *(scatter)* seeds in the field.

I took off my new **shoe** *(foot covering)* and tried to **shoo** *(frighten)* away the disgusting-looking bug.

As soon as the sun **shone** *(did shine)* over the horizon, I was **shown** *(guided)* to the cave that contained the diamonds.

Grab your camera so that you can **shoot** *(take)* a picture of all the kids sliding down the water **chute** *(narrow passage)*.

When the **side** *(edge)* of the statue didn't crack, the sculptor **sighed** *(exhaled in relief)* and said, "That marble is strong."

Dad always **sighs** *(exhales in regret)* when he sees the **size** *(great amount)* of my college tuition.

After you **slay** *(kill)* the dragon, jump into the **sleigh** *(horse-drawn sled)* and make your getaway.

The **slight** *(small)* magician was famous for his amazing **sleight**-of-hand *(quick small magic)* tricks.

How can such a little bird **soar** *(fly up very high)* like that without getting **sore** *(painful, hurting)* wings?

The creature **soared** *(flew high)* into the sky after snatching the **sword** *(weapon with blade)* from the warrior's hand.

You are now the **sole** *(only)* one who knows the secret; no other living **soul** *(person)* knows the solution to the mystery.

When the math teacher added up the figures in the column, she shouted, "**Some** *(quite a remarkable)* **sum** *(amount)*!"

The mother gave her **son** *(male child)* a hat to shield his eyes from the bright **sun** *(star Earth revolves around)*.

The **staid** *(dignified, serious)* lady **stayed** *(remained)* put until the man opened the door and said, "After you, ma'am."

There's a strange person sitting on the third **stair** *(step)*, but don't **stare** *(look directly)* at him, or he'll get embarrassed.

He sat down, leaned against a **stake** *(pole in the ground)*, took out his lunch, and ate his **steak** *(beef)* sandwich.

Remain **stationary** *(motionless)* in the crowded **stationery** *(writing supplies)* store so you don't break anything.

The bank vault is made of solid **steel** *(hard, strong metal)* so that no one can **steal** *(rob)* the money stored there.

The explorer sailed his boat **straight** *(directly)* through the perilous **strait** *(narrow channel of water)* and into the sea.

I was shown to my luxurious hotel **suite** *(connected rooms)* by a very **sweet** *(kind, gracious, courteous)* chambermaid.

When he **tacked** *(nailed)* a list of insults onto my bedroom door, he didn't show much **tact** *(sensitivity to what's proper)*.

Have you heard the **tale** *(story)* about the flying horse with the golden **tail** *(part that sticks out at the rear of an animal)*?

My camp counselor **taught** *(did teach)* me how to make my bed with very **taut** *(tight)* sheets.

The struggling artist couldn't believe that there was even a **tax** *(money paid to the government)* on **tacks** *(little nails)*.

If we beat this **team** *(group of players)* and win the finals, the streets will **teem** *(be crowded)* with our happy fans.

Her eyes started to **tear** *(fill with water)* when she saw that her expensive seat at the concert was in the last **tier** *(row)*.

Just because he drinks different kinds of **teas** *(hot flavored drinks)* doesn't mean that you should **tease** *(make fun of)* him.

The general grew **tense** *(nervous)* when he peered through his telescope at hundreds of enemy **tents** *(canvas shelters)*.

Their *(belongs to them)* e-mail said to put the money **there** *(in that place)*, but **they're** *(they are)* not here to get it.

She accidentally **threw** *(tossed)* the ball right **through** *(in one side, out the other)* her neighbor's bedroom window.

The wicked king was **thrown** *(hurled)* off his **throne** *(royal chair)* by the angry mob.

Add a little **thyme** *(sweet-smelling herb)* to the stew and put in back into the oven for a very short **time** *(period)*.

He **tied** *(fastened)* his little boat to the dock so it wouldn't float away with the **tide** *(change in sea level)*.

Go **to** *(toward)* the store, if you're not **too** *(overly)* tired, and get the cats **two** *(number after one)* bags of kitty litter.

The **toad** *(small animal like a frog)* put a rope around his favorite mushroom and **towed** *(dragged)* it to another forest.

The mechanic at the gas station stubbed his big **toe** *(part of the foot)* climbing into the old **tow** *(pull)* truck.

He **told** *(did tell)* of how the Liberty Bell had split while being **tolled** *(rung)* for the death of Chief Justice Marshall in 1835.

The **vane** *(pointer that shows wind direction)* blew off the roof and cut the **vein** *(blood vessel)* of the **vain** *(conceited)* man.

The wizard gave me a **vial** *(small bottle)* of **vile** *(awful-tasting)* potion and made me drink it as the lightning flashed.

Her husband didn't have a single **vice** *(bad habit)*, so she bought him a new **vise** *(clamping device)* for his workshop.

Don't **wade** *(walk)* into the sea until all your diving equipment has been **weighed** *(had its weight measured)*.

The mournful **wail** *(loud, sad cry)* of a lonely mermaid could make even a mighty **whale** *(large sea animal)* weep.

Eat less so your **waist** *(middle of body)* will get thinner, or all your dieting will be a **waste** *(worth nothing)*.

Our scale is broken, so you'll just have to **wait** *(be patient)* to find out your **weight** *(heaviness)*.

Did you **waive** *(give up)* all your rights to surf the world's greatest **wave** *(swell on the surface of water)*?

If this is the **way** *(manner)* they eat their **whey** *(curdled milk)*, they will soon **weigh** *(have weight)* more than they do now.

I caught a bad flu and felt very **weak** *(frail, sickly)* for over a **week** *(seven days)*.

The **weather** *(condition of the atmosphere)* is terrible, and I can't decide **whether** *(if)* or not to still have the barbecue.

The **wee** *(very tiny)* fairy told us that **we** *(you and I)* could have three magic wishes.

If we ever saw a **weed** *(harmful plant)* in our garden, **we'd** *(we would)* pull it out right away.

Where *(in what place)* did the carpenter **wear** *(be dressed in)* a costume made of hammers, saws, and other hard**ware** *(tools)*?

Which *(what particular one)* **witch** *(woman who practices sorcery)* at the Halloween party had the best costume?

He loves the look of **wood** *(what a tree is made of)* and **would** *(past of will)* like to build his whole house out of it.

She made **wry** *(humorous)* remarks while they were walking through a field of **rye** *(cereal grass)*.

On a farm I learned how to separate a **yolk** *(yellow part)* of an egg from the white part and put a **yoke** *(collar)* on oxen.

Homographs

If someone wrote *bow* on the blackboard, would you pronounce it to rhyme with *cow* or *go*? Either pronunciation would be correct. Words like that are called *homographs*. They have the same spelling but different sounds and meanings. You don't know how to pronounce these words until you see them in sentences.

Here are some common homographs in sentences to help you get them right. The words in quotation marks are rhyming words or pronunciation guides. The definitions are in italics.

For lunch, the **bass** (rhymes with "face"—*means low sound)* singer ate baked **bass** (rhymes with "class"—*means fish)*.

The archery champ took a **bow** ("go"—*curved weapon that shoots arrows)* and then a **bow** ("now"—*bending of body)*.

The wind began to **buffet** ("BUFF•it"—*hit against)* the tent as we lined up for the **buffet** ("buh•FAY"—*self-serve meal*).

Please **close** ("rose"—shut) the window that's **close** ("gross"—*near)* to the bed.

The bored guard will soon **desert** ("duh•ZERT"—*abandon)* his post in the **desert** ("DEZ•ert"—*hot, dry, sandy place)*.

Do ("glue") you know how to sing **do** ("go"—*first note on the musical scale)?*

The wildlife expert **does** ("fuzz"—*accomplishes)* his best to study **does** ("goes"—*female deer)* and other animals.

Did you see if it was a **dove** ("love"—*cooing bird)* or a pigeon that **dove** ("drove"—*did dive*) out of that tree?

The **drawer** ("DRAW•er"—*person who draws)* put some sketches in the **drawer** ("roar"—*sliding box in furniture)*.

He decorated the **entrance** ("EN•truns"—*way in)* so that it will **entrance** ("en•TRANS"—*delight)* all who visit.

The stationery store man will **lead** ("seed"—*show the way)* her to the **lead** ("bed"—*graphite)* pencils.

In **Lima** ("LEE•muh"—*capital city of Peru)*, some people eat **lima** ("I'm a"—*flat green beans)* beans with their dinners.

It's not easy to sleep if you **live** ("give"—*reside)* above a club that plays **live** ("hive"—*not recorded)* music all night.

In a **minute** ("spinet"—*60 seconds)* you'll see an amazing sight: a **minute** ("my newt"—*very small)* tap-dancing dog.

When the temperature fell to a number ("lumber"—*1, 2, 3, etc.)* below 0, my legs got number ("bummer"—*lost feeling).*

After his energy peaked ("sneeked"—*reached its maximum),* he started to look peaked ("PEE•kid"—*sickly).*

My Polish ("POLE•ish"—*from Poland)* friends sent me this bottle of great furniture polish ("abolish"—*shining cream).*

This primer ("swimmer"—*instruction book)* on paint, will help you apply primer ("timer"—*undercoat of paint)* to the wall.

I read ("seed"—*look at words)* a lot, but I can't always remember what I've read ("red"—*understood from reading).*

If the garbage dump is full, they'll refuse ("confuse"—*decline to accept)* the refuse ("REF•yoos"—*rubbish).*

After her break, she'll resume ("ruh•ZOOM"—*start to work again)* typing her resumé ("REZ•oo•may"—*list of jobs, etc.).*

Let's not have a row ("cow"—*quarrel, argument)* about who gets to row ("go"—*move boat through water with oars)* the boat first.

The sewer ("slower"—*one who sews)* of dresses slipped and fell into the sewer ("newer"—*underground waste pipe).*

The hungry sow ("cow"—*adult female hog)* was eating all the seeds we were trying to sow ("go"—*scatter seeds).*

When her brother tried to tear ("chair"—*rip)* up her picture, a tear ("deer"—*drop of water)* fell from her eye.

You may use ("news"—*utilize, put to use)* this thingamajig, if you can find any use ("goose"—*suitable purpose)* for it.

He tried to wind ("find"—*coil the spring of)* the steeple clock in the high wind ("pinned"—*moving air)* but almost fell.

The nurse **wound** ("found"—*wrapped*) a bandage around the soldier's **wound** ("spooned"—*injury*).

Confusing Words

Sometimes one word looks so much like another word that the words are easy to mix up. They sound alike, too, but not quite 100 percent alike. Here are some of the most confusing and misused words in English, in sentences that will help you use them correctly.

If you **accede** *(agree to)* to my request to borrow your car, I promise not to **exceed** *(go faster than)* the speed limit.

Grandma would never **accept** *(receive)* presents **except** *(other than)* for ones her grandchildren made themselves.

To succeed, **adopt** *(follow)* a plan, **adapt** *(adjust)* to your new job, and become **adept** *(skilled)* at computer skills.

The team was **all ready** *(completely prepared)* to play, but the game had **already** *(before this time)* been forfeited.

All together *(everyone at once)* now, singers, let's be **altogether** *(totally)* wonderful in the concert.

Don't **allude** *(refer to, make mention of)* to the time he tried to **elude** *(evade, escape from)* blame for what he had done.

My **ally** *(friend)* and I ran into the **alley** *(narrow passageway)* chasing the truck with the stolen **alloy** *(mixture of metals)*.

The jungle doctor told a fascinating **anecdote** *(story)* about her discovery of the **antidote** *(remedy)* for snake bites.

A beam of golden light shot out at an odd **angle** *(slant)* from the cloud, and an **angel** *(messenger from heaven)* appeared.

"**Anyway** *(in any event)*," I said, "**any way** *(by whatever means)* that you decorate the house will be fine with us."

He told the tale of his **ascent** *(climb up)* of Mount Everest in a heavy foreign **accent** *(the way words are pronounced)*.

A **bibliography** *(list of books)* of the lives of great scientists must include the **biography** *(life story)* of Sir Isaac Newton.

When you **breathe** *(inhale)* in this country air, you can be sure that not a single **breath** *(inhaled air)* contains pollutants.

If you omit every **comma** *(punctuation mark)*, your teacher will think you're in a punctuation **coma** *(state of unconsciousness)*.

I must **commend** *(praise)* you, General, on the excellent way you **command** *(manage and control)* your troops.

You are my trusted **confidant** *(close friend)*, so I am **confident** *(certain)* you will never reveal my secrets.

My **conscience** *(awareness of what's right)* bothers me, for I am **conscious** *(aware)* of the fact that I have done wrong.

The **consul** *(government foreign service officer)* spoke to the foreign **council** *(assembly of people)* and offered them good **counsel** *(advice and guidance)*.

The **continuous** *(never stopping)* rain and the **continual** *(stopping and starting)* floods caused a calamity.

I'm pleased by the **cooperation** *(working together)* between my office and your **corporation** *(company)*.

It is the **custom** *(usually practice)* in my country to wear this festive **costume** *(clothing)* for celebrations.

This is **decent** *(acceptable, fairly good)* weather for the **descent** *(climb down)* of the mountain, but if asked to do it on a pogo stick, I must **dissent** *(say no)*.

When she was in the **desert** *(dry, sandy place),* she dreamed of her favorite **dessert** *(end-of-meal dish)*, ice cream.

Is the **diseased** *(infected)* patient who was brought in last night still alive or sadly **deceased** *(dead)*?

What **effect** *(result)* do you think her angry speech had on the election? Did it **affect** *(change)* the vote?

The secret police could not **elicit** *(draw out)* any facts from the spy about her **illicit** *(illegal)* activities.

My uncle **emigrated** *(left a country)* from Russia and **immigrated** *(entered a country to live)* to the United States.

The **eminent** *(distinguished)* space scientist announced the **imminent** *(about to happen)* discovery of a new solar system.

Father *(dad)* traveled **farther** *(more distance)* to do **further** *(more)* research for the book he was writing.

Finally *(at last),* you should add **finely** *(in very small pieces)* chopped nuts to the cake batter and stir thoroughly.

In the job I had **formerly** *(in the past)*, I was **formally** *(in an official manner)* introduced to the king at a state banquet.

You aren't **human** *(relating to human beings)* if you don't have **humane** *(compassionate)* feelings when you see sad things.

Was it only an **illusion** *(misleading idea)* or did the speaker make a scary **allusion** *(reference)* to devils and monsters?

Your story is so incredible *(unbelievable)*, can you blame me for being incredulous *(doubtful, disbelieving)*?

Who knew that such an ingenuous *(simple, unsophisticated)* boy could think of such an ingenious *(clever, brilliant)* plan?

Of the two magicians we discussed, the former disappeared immediately, and the latter *(the second mentioned)* levitated later *(afterward)*.

You look tired, so lay *(put down)* your suitcases on the table and lie *(put yourself at rest)* down on the sofa for a nap.

She will surely lose *(not win)* the race if her sneakers are too loose *(not tied tightly)*.

The well-known steel magnate *(powerful, influential business leader)* was a magnet *(strong attraction)* for publicity.

If the general behaves in a moral *(good, ethical, virtuous)* way, it will lift the morale *(attitude, spirits)* of the army.

Anything written about you in your files in the personnel *(employee)* office is supposed to be personal *(private)*.

At the World Series, I took a great picture *(photograph)* of the pitcher *(player who throws the ball)* on the mound.

Precede *(go in front of)* me so that you can proceed *(go forward)* to the school bus before it leaves.

Here's the teacher's proposition *(suggested plan)*: Learn what a preposition *(part of speech)* is, and she'll give you an A.

The government will prosecute *(take criminal court action against)* anyone who tries to persecute *(treat cruelly)* you.

The baby-sitter shouted, "Either these kids remain **quite** *(completely)* **quiet** *(peaceful, still)*, or I **quit** *(leave my job)*!"

Every time I **raise** *(pull up)* the flag, my patriotic spirits **rise** *(go higher)*.

Every soldier in the **regiment** *(military unit)* had to follow a strict **regimen** *(regulated system)* of diet and exercise.

Along this very **route** *(road, course, way)*, the retreating army suffered its greatest **rout** *(tremendous defeat)*.

Guards, **seize** *(capture)* that noisy canary and make it **cease** *(stop)* its annoying chirping.

Set *(put down)* your books on the bench, child, and **sit** *(rest your lower body)* in that comfortable chair by the fire.

Then *(at that time)* he had the nerve to tell me that he was smarter **than** *(compared to)* Einstein.

The detective walked **through** *(from one end to the other)* the crime scene making a **thorough** *(complete)* list of the clues.

Driving this **tortuous** *(winding, twisting)* road at night in the rain was a **torturous** *(painful)* experience for the new driver.

The **umpire** *(official judge in a sport)* has refereed games all over the British **empire** *(group of countries under one rule)*.

Are people who live in **urban** *(city)* areas more **urbane** *(sophisticated, refined)* that those who live in the country?

To be perfectly **veracious** *(honest)*, he has a **voracious** *(hoggish)* appetite, so don't leave him alone in your kitchen.

EXTRA

There are thirty-nine homonym mistakes in the following sentence about the zoo. Can you find them all? (Remember, all of the wrong words are spelled correctly.)

Last summer at the zoo wee saw a dough (that's a female dear) berry some buries under a Cyprus tree; a grisly bare with gray fir and sharp clause; a hair with tiny feat eating a karat; a hoarse with a flowing main on the bridal path; a pear of links with large pause; a heard of news under a beach tree; plenty of foul squawking and gobbling; sum insects (like an aunt, a be, and a flee) that flue buy; a wild bore with a strong cent; a stubborn borough; a you or too; and a blew wail splashing its tale. Those daze at the zoo were grate!

Here is the same paragraph with all the right homonyms:

Last summer at the zoo we saw a doe (that's a female deer) bury some berries under a cypress tree; a grizzly bear with gray fur and sharp claws; a hare with tiny feet eating a carrot; a horse with a flowing mane on the bridle path; a pair of lynx with large paws; a herd of gnus under a beech tree; plenty of fowl squawking and gobbling; some insects (like an ant, a bee, and a flea) that flew by; a wild boar with a strong scent; a stubborn burro; a ewe or two; and a blue whale splashing its tail. Those days at the zoo were great!

chapter 4

Word Families

Happiness

Happiest

Happily

Happier

the HAPPY FAMILY

Words can belong to families, just as people do. A word family is a group of words that all come from the same source. That's how they're "related." Knowing about word families can help you figure out the meaning of a new word if it's related to a word you already know. For example, here's a beautiful word family.

beauty, beautiful, beautifully, beautify

These words came from the Latin word for "pretty," *bellus,* but each word is a different part of speech.

How you can tell the part of speech of a specific word in a word family? By how it's being used.

If it names a person, place, thing, or idea, it's a noun.
If it shows action, it's a verb.
If it describes a noun, it's an adjective.
If it tells how the verb shows action, it's an adverb. (An adverb can also describe an adjective.)

Beauty is a noun because it names an idea.

Grandmother tries to bring beauty into the world.

What idea does grandmother try to bring into the world? Beauty.

Beautify is a verb because it shows action.

Grandmother beautifies the neighborhood by planting flowers up and down the street.

What does she do to the neighborhood? She beautifies it.

Beautiful is an adjective because it describes a noun.

Grandmother is a beautiful woman.

How do you describe grandmother? Beautiful.

Beautifully is an adverb because it answers the question "How is the verb showing action?"

Grandmother can sing ballads beautifully.

How does she sing? Beautifully.

Now you can see that a word family can include a noun, a verb, an adjective, and an adverb, and all the words come from the same original word.

Here are some other common word families.

Noun	My classroom is full of good cheer.
Verb	I'm going to try to cheer up my sad friend.
Adjective	I got a cheerful card from my cousin today.
Adverb	The baby was gurgling cheerfully in her crib.

Noun	This is a tough decision to make.
Verb	I can't decide what to wear tonight.
Adjective	Her decisive actions saved the day!
Adverb	We must all act decisively in this matter.

Noun	Her story was just one big falsehood.
Verb	The kid falsified his age on the job application.
Adjective	Did you give a false name when you came in?
Adverb	They testified falsely that they weren't there.

Noun	Your explanation brought clarity to this confusing situation.
Verb	Can you clarify what you mean, because I'm not sure I understand?
Adjective	These instructions are clear and easy to follow.
Adverb	I can hear you clearly over the phone even though you are thousands of miles away.

Noun	Let your imagination soar!
Verb	Just imagine what you could do with the money.
Adjective	That's an imaginative solution to the problem.
Adverb	His dorm room was decorated imaginatively.

Noun	The lightness of the bubbles kept them afloat.
Verb	If your suitcase is too heavy, I'll lighten it.
Adjective	I'm not so hungry, so I'll just have a light snack.
Adverb	Step lightly so you don't wake the baby.

Noun	This strong magnet will pick up all those nails.
Verb	Mom magnetizes all our pictures to the refrigerator.
Adjective	My favorite teacher has a magnetic personality.
Adverb	They were magnetically drawn to each other.

Noun	We packed everything to get ready for our move.
Verb	The dancers moved very gracefully.
Adjective	The patio furniture was light and movable.
Adverb	The ambassador spoke movingly about the need for peace between the two countries.

Noun	We are studying the origin of life on Earth.
Verb	Who originated the idea of homework, anyway?
Adjective	This is the original oil painting, not a copy.
Adverb	Originally he was a dancer; now he's a singer.
Noun	It was a pleasure meeting you, sir.
Verb	My clean room will shock and please my mother.
Adjective	This sauce has a surprisingly pleasant taste.
Adverb	The bed was pleasingly soft to the tired man.
Noun	The mayor was skilled in politics.
Verb	The angry debate politicized the people.
Adjective	They shouldn't make recess a political issue.
Adverb	His actions are always politically motivated.
Noun	I'd really like some peace and quiet around here.
Verb	The librarian tried in vain to quiet the noisy kids.
Adjective	It's quiet in the pet store when the mice are asleep.
Adverb	He lived quietly in a little cottage in the woods.
Noun	I always try to show reverence to my elders.
Verb	My whole class just revered our math teacher.
Adjective	She made a reverent speech at the ceremony.
Adverb	We treat our grandparents reverently.
Noun	Show your sister a little tenderness sometimes.
Verb	Pound the meat with this hammer to tenderize it.
Adjective	Waiter, I'd like a very tender chicken, please.
Adverb	The child kissed him tenderly on the cheek.

Here is a sentence that contains all four members of one word family. Can you tell what part of speech each word is?

He *expressed* himself so *expressively* that everyone loved his *expressive expressions*.

Verb   expressed (shows action)
Adverb   expressively (tells how he expressed himself)
Adjective   expressive (describes his expressions)
Noun   expressions (things)

Using Context Clues

t's always a good idea to have a dictionary nearby when you sit down to read. You just never know when an author is going to throw a word at you that you don't know.

But there are times when the dictionary is on the other side of the room, or you're someplace where there is no dictionary, or maybe you just don't want to slow the flow by looking up a word right then. There's still a good way to figure out the meaning of a word: use context clues. The context of a word includes all the other words, phrases, clauses, and sentences around it. These may contain clues that can help you guess what the word means.

Context, context, "Context context context context context context," context word context context, context context context; context context context context: context context!

For instance, suppose somebody painted borborygmus on a wall. What does it mean? You don't have a clue. No words surround it to give you the faintest hint.

But if you saw *borborygmus* in some kind of context, you might have a fighting chance to figure it out. So let's put it into a context.

My Most Embarrassing Moment in School

I was so nervous about the big test that I hadn't eaten all day. There I was, in a perfectly silent room, with about 50 other kids, and suddenly my stomach embarrassed me. Everyone could hear my borborygmus as clearly as if a freight train had rumbled by. And it wouldn't stop. I coughed to cover the sound, but the kid next to me told me to be quiet. I was never so humiliated in my life. Even the A+ I got on the test couldn't take away my mortification.

Did you spot the clues? The author was embarrassed by his empty stomach. People could hear a rumbling sound. Now what do you think *borborygmus* means? If you look it up in an advanced dictionary, you'll see that its definition is

"the rumbling, gurgling noise of gas moving through the intestines."

That can definitely be embarrassing. (Just in case you want to use this word in conversation, it's pronounced "bor•buh•RIG•mus.")

Let's try figuring out the meanings of more strange words from their contexts.

She'd never experienced horripilation before, but when her brother hid in her closet and started making scary sounds in the middle of the night, her hair just stood up on the back of her neck.

Clues: "scary" . . . "hair stood up"

horripilation: the bristling or standing on end of a person's hair when he or she is frightened

One morning in 1654, Lord George arose early, pulled on his baggy galligaskins, and went to investigate why the cats were howling so loudly.

Clues: "1654" . . . "Lord —" . . . "pulled on" . . . "baggy"

galligaskins: loose-fitting trousers or hose worn in the 16th and 17th centuries, chiefly British

I was reading about how, in the old days, if you were bad in school, teachers would hit you right on your hands with a ferule. I'm so glad that now all they do is make you stay after school.

Clues: "old days" . . . "bad in school" . . . "hit"

ferule: a flat stick, cane, or piece of wood that was once used to hit young students on their hands to punish them

While he was sight-seeing in the jungles of Brazil, my cousin almost died when a jararacussu slithered out from under a rock without warning and bit him on the leg. That could have ruined his vacation. Luckily, they got him to a hospital in time, and the doctors got the poison out.

Clues: "Brazil" . . . "almost died" . . . "slithered out" . . . "poison"

jararacussu: a poisonous Brazilian snake

Of course, the words in the paragraphs above are not your everyday, normal kind of words. They are especially hard, and most adults probably wouldn't know them. But if you came close to figuring out what those words meant from their contexts, you can figure out other, more normal, words that you might see when there's no dictionary within a hundred miles.

Here are more vocabulary words to practice your context clue skills on. These are more common than the ones above.

He couldn't figure out why his sister was in such a foul mood. She was obviously furious about something and picked a fight with him over nothing. But when she found out that it was her cat that had knocked the yogurt onto her history homework, not her brother, she stopped being so belligerent and went back to being her plain old bratty, silly self.

belligerent: eager to fight; hostile, aggressive; quarrelsome

Luckily she was ambidextrous, so even when she broke her right hand playing basketball, she could still do her homework with her left hand.

ambidextrous: able to use both hands equally well.

At first they thought it was an apparition emerging from the shadows in the cemetery, but then they realized it was only the caretaker coming to find out who was there in the middle of the night.

apparition: a ghostly figure, a phantom

Hamlet stood by himself on the stage, expressing his deepest thoughts in the famous soliloquy, "To be or not to be."

soliloquy: a speech in a play in which a character, when alone, reveals his or her thoughts

Now that you've learned all the strange words in this chapter by using context clues, here's a little story to practice your new vocabulary knowledge on.

The frightened young actor thought for sure that the belligerent director would whack him with two ferules (one in his left hand and one in his right, for the director was ambidextrous) if he disturbed the audience with his borborygmus while delivering the famous soliloquy, so he stood there in his new galligaskins wishing that a jararacussu would slip into the theater and bite the director, who would then become merely a harmless apparition.

chapter 6

How to Use a Dictionary

What's in a Dictionary?

Of all the gazillions of books in the world, a dictionary is one of the most useful. It doesn't have an exciting plot or many interesting characters, but it does give you all sorts of important information about words: how to spell them, how to pronounce them, what they mean, and more.

Here are some sample dictionary entries.

Entry word   Part of speech

big (big) *adjective* 1. Large in size. *What big eyes you have!* 2. Of great importance. *I have some big news for you.*

Pronunciation   Shows how word is used.

toy (toi) 1. *noun* A plaything. 2. *verb* To amuse oneself; to play. *Mia likes to toy around with the idea of traveling around the world. Sam toyed with the rubber band.* 3. *adjective* Miniature. *Have you ever seen a toy poodle?*

Syllable Break   Numbers appear when the word has more than one definition.

un·cut (un·KUT) *adjective* 1. Not cut: *uncut hair.* 2. In a natural state before shaping and polishing: *uncut diamond.*

So remember to pack your dictionary the next time you have to take a long car ride or you plan to get stranded on a deserted island. It will give you plenty of fascinating things to read about.

Entry Words

Entry words are the main words in a dictionary. They're the words you're looking for. They are always listed alphabetically. To make them stand out on the page, they are printed in **bold-face** and sometimes in a bigger size, or a different font (type-face), or a different color from the rest of the words.

Alphabetical Order

Since the entry words in a dictionary are listed alphabetically, it is really important for you to know all the 26 letters of the English alphabet in order.

Most dictionaries are many hundreds of pages long, so to make the job of finding a word easier, think of a dictionary in three parts.

Part 1:   Letters a to f (a b c d e f)
Part 2:   Letters g to p (g h i j k l m n o p)
Part 3:   Letters q to z (q r s t u v w x y z)

To help you remember the three parts of a dictionary, here are three alphabetical-order sentences.

Part 1 (a to f):
A brave cat doesn't ever faint.

Part 2 (g to p):
Giggling happily in July, kangaroos love munching noisily on plants.

Part 3 (q to z):
Queen Roslyn said that ugly veterinarians will x-ray your zebra.

Now, when you want to look up words that begin with a, b, c, d, e, or f, turn to the first third of the dictionary.

Words that begin with g, h, i, j, k, l, m, n, o, or p will be in the middle third.

You'll find words starting with all the rest of the letters (q, r, s, t, u, v, w, x, y, z) in the last third.

Guide Words

Two guide words appear at the top of pages in a dictionary. The first guide word tells you the first word on that page. The second guide word tells you the last word on that page.

If the word you're looking for is on a certain page, it will come after the first guide word and before the second guide word in alphabetical order. Guide words save you a lot of time because you don't have to look up and down many pages to find the right page.

As you flip through a dictionary looking for a specific entry word, look at the guide words. Just as a guide at the zoo might say, "A mockingbird is in this cage," the guide words mistletoe-modern say, "Mockingbird is on this page."

In a few dictionaries, there may be only one guide word per page. As you look at two open pages, the guide word on the top left is the first word on the left page. The guide word on the top right is the last word on the right page.

Entry Word You're Looking For	Guide Words to Help You Find It	Because the Alphabetical Order Is
cucumber	crystal - culprit	crystal, cucumber, culprit
earmuffs	eagle - earthworm	eagle, earmuffs, earthworm
jellyfish	jeans - jigsaw	jeans, jellyfish, jigsaw

Pronunciation

Syllables

A syllable is a unit of a word that makes up one uninterrupted sound. Seeing how a word is broken into syllables will help you pronounce and spell it more easily. Dictionaries separate the entry words into syllables with dots, hyphens, or spaces:

dic•tion•ar•y   dic-tion-ar-y   dic tion ar y

Phonetic Alphabet and Regular Letters

Words in English are not always pronounced the way they look. Some dictionaries help you know the correct pronunciation of an entry word by spelling it out using the phonetic alphabet, regular and funny-looking letters with marks on top like ¯, ^, or ˇ. Other dictionaries use just regular letters with no symbols or marks.

The spellings that show pronunciation usually come in parentheses right after the entry words, but some dictionaries put them into brackets or between slash marks.

chim•pan•zee (chim´ pan zē)
chim pan zee [chim´•pan•zē´]
chim-pan-zee \chim-pan-´zē\
chim pan zee \chim´ pan zē´ or chim pan´ zē\
chim•pan•zee (*chim*-pan-**zee** or chim-**pan**-zee)

Pronunciation Keys

Because not all dictionaries use the same symbols, dictionaries have pronunciation keys that show you how to pronounce the letters and symbols in that book. Always check the pronunciation key to figure out how to pronounce a new word.

Here are some examples of symbols you might see in a pronunciation key. The sample words show how the symbols are pronounced.

Symbol	Sample Words
ă	hat, bad
ā	age, paid, ray
ä	father, bother, cart, heart
â	air, care, bear, their
ĕ	let, pleasure, said, friend, any
ē	be, easy, feet, piece, key
ĭ	it, English, busy
ī	ride, lie, buy
î	dear, fierce
ŏ	hot, horrible, watch
ō	go, oat, toe, though
ô	for, paw, taught, all

ŭ	up, flood, double, love
ū	use, cue
u̇	put, wood
ü	rule, truth
kw	choir, quick
ng	thing, pink
th	thin, bath
th	then, mother
zh	vision, pleasure, azure

Schwa ə

In many pronunciation keys, you might see a funny-looking letter that looks like an upside down *e*. This symbol is called a schwa.

Schwa is usually pronounced like a soft "uh," in syllables that are not stressed. Any vowel (*a, e, i, o,* or *u*) can be represented with a schwa. Say the following words aloud to yourself and you'll see how to sound out a schwa.

Schwa for a around (ə round)	Schwa for e taken (ta kən)
Schwa for i pencil (pen səl)	Schwa for o lemon (lem ən)
Schwa for u circus (ser kəs)	

As you see, when you pronounce a word with a schwa, you speak the schwa sound ("uh") softly and kind of slur over it. You definitely do not stress the syllable with the schwa in it.

Hippopotamus has three schwas in it: hip' ə pot' ə məs.

Accented Syllables

In some words, one syllable gets stressed more than the others. You're supposed to say that syllable more loudly or more strongly. Some dictionaries print the accented syllables in bold-face or capital letters.

monster (mon stur) or (MON stur)

Other dictionaries put an accent mark that looks something like an apostrophe before or after the syllable that you say with more force.

monster (mon' stər)

Some longer words (three or more syllables) have two stressed syllables, a stronger one and a lighter one. Some dictionaries use a lighter and darker accent mark to show how to stress the syllables.

tyrannosaur (ti•ran'•ə•sor')

Other dictionaries put the more lightly stressed syllable in italics and the more heavily stressed syllable in boldface.

tyrannosaur (ti-ran-uh-sor)

Different Pronunciations

Some words have more than one acceptable pronunciation, and your dictionary will show you all of them.

adult (uh•DUHLT) or (AH•duhlt)
bouquet (boh•KAY) or (boo•KAY)
detail (di•TAYL) or (DEE•tayl)

Glossary

A glossary is a mini-dictionary. It's not a whole book; it's a few pages in the back of a book. It doesn't have thousands and thousands of general words on all subjects. The words defined in a glossary are specialized words that relate to the specific subject of the book it's in.

Here are a few sample listings that you might find in some glossaries.

Glossary of Math Terms (pre-algebra and geometry)

abscissa The first number in the ordered pair for a point in the coordinate plane.

absolute value The absolute value of a number is its distance from 0 on a number line; the number itself.

acute angle An angle that has a measure less than 90° but greater than 0°.

acute triangle A triangle made up of three acute angles.

addend A number that is added.

angle Two rays with a single endpoint, called the vertex.

arc A part of a circle.

area The measure of a plane region in terms of square units.

Glossary of Social Studies Terms

baby boom The sudden, sharp increase in the birthrate in the United States after World War II, from 1947 to about 1961.

balance of trade The difference in value between the goods exported from and imported into a country during a specific period of time.

bicameral A legislature with two chambers, branches, or houses.

blacklist A list of persons, organizations, or workers that subjected themselves to disapproval or suspicion because of their actions and are boycotted or otherwise punished.

Black Power A movement that emphasized racial pride and expressed an increased drive by African-Americans to win civil rights and control over their own lives through the creation of their own political and cultural institutions.

blitzkrieg A German word for "lightning war," a swift, sudden military offensive, usually by combined air and mobile land forces.

blockade To close off a coast to prevent ships entering or leaving the ports.

border states Slave states (Delaware, Maryland, Virginia, Kentucky, and Missouri) located on the line next to free states of the North during the Civil War.

Glossary of Science Words

calorie The amount of energy (unit of heat) needed to raise the temperature of one kilogram of water by one Celsius degree.

capillary A tiny blood vessel where substances are exchanged between the blood and the body cells.

carbohydrate An organic compound made of carbon, hydrogen, and oxygen that serves as an energy source in the diets of animals.

chemical bond The force that holds two atoms together in a molecule or crystal.

cholesterol A waxy lipid (like fat, oil, wax) that is found in all animal cells.

compound A substance that is made of two or more elements or parts chemically combined.

condensation The change from a gas or vapor to a liquid.

Glossary of Names in Ancient Greek and Roman Stories

Daedelus A legendary Greek inventor and builder of the Labyrinth; he made wings to enable himself and his son Icarus to escape from imprisonment.

Demeter The Greek goddess of agriculture. Roman name: Ceres.

Dido Legendary queen of Carthage who fell in love with Aeneas, defender of Troy.

Dionysus The Greek god of wine. Roman name: Bacchus.

Dis The god of the lower world; also called Pluto and Hades.

EXTRA

Dictionaries have been printed in the form of books for hundreds of years. But today you can also get handheld electronic dictionaries. There are also several dictionaries you can access over the Internet.

For links to more than 700 on-line dictionaries and glossaries, go to

www.onelook.com/index.html

Some other good Web sites for people interested in words and building up their vocabularies are

www.vocabulary.com

www.dictionary.com

www.thesaurus.com/Roget-Alpha-Index.html

www.yourdictionary.com

www.itools.com/research-it

www.word-detective.com/backidx.html

www.merriam-webster.com

chapter 7

How to Use a Thesaurus

Synonyms and Antonyms

SIMILAR

OPPOSITES

Because there are so many words in English, some words mean the same thing as or the opposite of other words.

Synonyms are words that have the same or nearly the same meanings.

Antonyms are words that have opposite or nearly opposite meanings.

(To help you remember which is which, remember that synonym and same both begin with s.)

Because there are so many synonyms and antonyms in English, you have many choices of how to express yourself. But where do you find synonyms and antonyms of words? In a thesaurus (pronounced "thuh-SORE-us").

What Is a Thesaurus and How Do You Use It?

A thesaurus is a book that contains lists of synonyms and sometimes antonyms.

The word *thesaurus* comes from the Latin word *thesaurus*, which means "treasury." So a thesaurus is a treasury of words. Some publishers don't use the word *thesaurus*. They call their books dictionaries of synonyms and antonyms. They're the same as thesauruses.

There are thesauruses for writers of all ages. The bigger and more advanced a thesaurus is, the more words it contains.

You'll find the most common, everyday words and those that are less familiar and more sophisticated.

However, some college-level thesauruses can be complicated to use because of the small print and the way the words are arranged. So it's a good idea to get a thesaurus that's appropriate for your age and grade.

One kind of thesaurus that's easy to use has main entry words arranged alphabetically, like a dictionary. These are followed by common synonyms and antonyms. It's also helpful to have a simple alphabetical index that lists all the synonyms and antonyms in the book. If you don't find the word you're looking for under the main entry words, just look in the index. If the word is not there, think of another word that means about the same thing and look that word up. Keep trying, and you'll find what you want.

Who Is Roget?

On the cover of many thesauruses you may see the name Roget (pronounced row-ZHAY). Peter Mark Roget was a British doctor and scholar. In 1852, he published the world's first thesaurus.

Cross-references

A cross-reference tells you to look in another part of the book to find more information related to what you're trying to find. The word *see* is usually used for cross-references.

For instance, if you look up the word *job* in a thesaurus, you might be given synonyms like *task, chore, errand,* and *work,* and the cross-reference *"see FUNCTION, DUTY, WORK."*

By following all the cross-references, you'll find all the possible words you need to help you make the perfect choice for what you're writing (like *office, responsibility, obligation, labor, toil, effort,* and *drudgery*).

Thesaurus + Dictionary = The Perfect Word

Sometimes a thesaurus by itself is not enough to find the exact synonym or antonym you need. So keep a dictionary nearby to check the definitions of the words you find in your thesaurus.

A Nice Example

Suppose you are writing a story about a person who is nice. *Nice* is a nice word, but it's not too descriptive or exciting. Actually, *nice* can be a kind of boring word.

So, go to your nearest thesaurus and look up *nice*. Wow! Look at all the words that mean the same thing as *nice*: *pleasant, likeable, agreeable, good-natured, friendly, kind, sociable, cordial, neighborly, genial, proper, well-behaved, charming, delightful, gracious, amiable, affable, convivial, amicable, approachable, congenial, personable,* and more.

Which word should you use? Choose one of the words and look it up in your dictionary to see if it means exactly what you want it to mean.

Suppose that in your story, your nice person meets a person who is not nice. How can you find a word to describe that character? If your thesaurus has antonyms, look in it for antonyms of *nice*.

You'll find words like *unpleasant, coarse, unscrupulous, rude, rough, nasty, disagreeable, obnoxious, wretched, terrible, dreadful, hateful, evil, wicked, naughty, offensive, unprincipled, villainous, detestable, deplorable, reprehensible, mean-spirited, cantankerous, mean, ornery,* and more.

Choose one of those words and look it up in a dictionary to make sure it's the word that describes the not nice character in your story perfectly.

If your thesaurus doesn't have antonyms, think of any word that's the opposite of *nice* and look for synonyms of that word.

You can find synonyms and antonyms in places other than just thesauruses. Many regular dictionaries give synonyms and antonyms along with definitions. Look for the abbreviations **syn.** and **ant.** Many word processing programs and hand-held electronic dictionaries have built-in thesauruses with synonyms and antonyms.

Shades of Meaning

Just as one color can have different shades, like *pink* (pale red), *scarlet* (bright red with a little orange), *crimson* (deep, vivid red with a little purple), *maroon* (dark, purplish-brownish red), and *vermilion* (vivid, orange red), words can have "shades of meaning."

Sometimes a word that you think means exactly the same thing as another word really doesn't. There may be a slight degree of difference between the meanings. These shades of meaning can sometimes be important.

Let's imagine you're writing a story about a cold day. *Cold* means "having a low temperature." But exactly how cold is the day in your story? Cold enough so that you need a scarf? Cold enough to make your teeth chatter? Cold enough to freeze your eyelashes?

In a thesaurus you will find these synonyms for *cold: cool, chilly, wintry, frosty, icy, freezing, frigid, arctic,* and *Siberian.*

They all refer to different degrees of cold.

cool: neither very hot nor very cold
chilly: cold enough to make you shiver
wintry: characteristic of winter; cold
frosty: covered with frost (small ice crystals)
freezing: to be at or below the temperature at which ice
forms (32° Fahrenheit or 0° Celsius)
icy: covered with ice; bitterly cold; freezing
frigid: exceedingly cold
arctic: intensely cold; frigid (The Arctic is near the North
Pole.)
Siberian: fiercely cold (Siberia is a remote region of
Russia that is known for its long, frigid winters.)

So the wintry day in your story could start off cool, then get chillier, become frosty, and end up frigid. Your freezing readers will feel as if they were in Siberia or the Arctic. They'll have to wear gloves to turn the pages. *Brrr!*

Use your dictionary to be aware of the shades of meaning between words. That way you'll use exactly the words you want, to describe perfectly what you're writing about.

Parts of Speech

You also need to be careful about parts of speech. Synonyms of verbs should be verbs. Synonyms of nouns should be nouns.

Avoiding Repeats

Knowing more than one way to say something can be very useful when you want to repeat an idea, but you don't want to repeat words. Think about the paragraph that follows.

When Jennifer got her hard science test back, she was happy because she had gotten a good grade. Happy, she showed her parents the good grade on the hard test. Her mom was happy that she had gotten such a good grade on such a hard test. Her dad was happy that she had gotten such a good grade on such a hard test. When her happy parents bought her the CD she wanted for getting such a good grade on such a hard test, she was very happy.

Here's how that paragraph would look with synonyms replacing *hard*, *happy*, and *good* after the first sentence.

When Jennifer got her hard science test back, she was happy because she had gotten a good grade. Joyful, she showed her parents the fine grade on the difficult test. Her mom was delighted that she had gotten an outstanding grade on such a tough test. Her dad was elated that she had gotten a splendid grade on the demanding test. When her jubilant parents bought her the CD she wanted for getting an excellent grade on such a formidable test, she was ecstatic.

A String of Synonyms

Sometimes, to emphasize something strongly, you may want to use a whole string of synonyms in a row.

Suppose a person in the story you're writing does something really stupid, and his friend shouts, "That was stupid, stupid, stupid!" It might be much more dramatic if the furious friend shouts:

"That was scatterbrained, featherbrained, and birdbrained!" or "That was empty-headed, muddleheaded, and blockheaded!"

You can't use words in a row like that too often, but when you do, it can be powerful writing. And you'll find the powerful words in your thesaurus.

Mini-Thesaurus for Adjectives

Here are some synonyms and antonyms for 80 adjectives that you might want to use in your writing. There are many more synonyms and antonyms for adjectives, nouns, verbs, prepositions, and adverbs in a full thesaurus.

	Synonyms	Antonyms
adult	grown-up, mature, full-grown, ripe, fully developed	immature, adolescent, young, babyish, infantile, green, inexperienced, juvenile, puerile, sophomoric, unripe, undeveloped
alert	attentive, wide-awake, watchful, vigilant, aware, observant	inattentive, asleep, drowsy, dozing, oblivious
alive	living, animate, animated, vital, active, existing	dead, extinct, deceased, expired
alone	lone, solitary, isolated, unaccompanied, solo, secluded, separate, apart, detached, removed	accompanied, chaperoned, attended

	Synonyms	Antonyms
angry	cross, upset, fussy, grouchy, irritable, cranky, mad, furious, annoyed, irritated, aggravated, exasperated, incensed, enraged	peaceful, placid, tranquil, quiet, unruffled, composed, serene, patient
awful	terrible, horrible, dreadful, appalling, frightful, repulsive, offensive, disgusting	pleasant, pleasing, attractive, inviting, delightful, charming, agreeable, lovely
bad	wicked, evil, sinful, vile, mischievous, sinister, harmful, destructive, pernicious, malevolent, malicious	admirable, commendable, exceptional, worthy, excellent, meritorious
big	large, huge, enormous, vast, immense, gigantic, colossal, tremendous, massive, titanic, mammoth, monumental	little, small, minute, tiny, miniature, petite, diminutive, short, lilliputian
boring	dull, uninteresting, tedious, monotonous, tiresome, blah, humdrum, wearisome, fatiguing	interesting, exciting, fascinating, absorbing, engaging, appealing, entertaining, intriguing, engrossing

	Synonyms	Antonyms
brave	fearless, daring, defiant, bold, courageous, heroic, stalwart, intrepid, audacious, dauntless	afraid, scared, fearful, frightened, terrified, timid, petrified, apprehensive, fainthearted
bright	brilliant, glowing, shiny, radiant, sunny, glaring, beaming, glistening	dull, pale, pallid, drab, colorless, gloomy, dim, sober, somber, dingy
calm	peaceful, serene, tranquil, placid, still, unruffled, sedate, composed	wild, agitated, stormy, untamed, savage, frenzied, turbulent, riotous, boisterous
careful	painstaking, thorough, exact, cautious, prudent, watchful, wary, vigilant	careless, negligent, thoughtless, reckless, heedless, neglectful
clumsy	awkward, ungainly, gawky, lumbering	dexterous, skillful, expert
comfortable	cozy, snug, cushy, sheltered, soft	uncomfortable, miserable, discomforting
common	ordinary, typical, familiar, everyday, average, normal, customary, usual, widespread	rare, extraordinary, exceptional, odd, uncommon, unusual, strange, bizarre

	Synonyms	Antonyms
complete	full, total, whole, entire	incomplete, deficient, inadequate, lacking, imperfect, unfinished
curious	inquisitive, interested, nosy, prying, spying, peeping, meddlesome	uninterested, aloof, indifferent, detached, unconcerned, bored
dark	gloomy, dusky, dim, unlit,	bright, brilliant, glaring, dazzling
deadly	fatal, mortal, lethal, malignant, virulent, killing	vital, invigorating, strengthening
delicious	tasty, appetizing, luscious, savory, palatable, delectable, scrumptious, yummy	distasteful, unsavory, bitter, unpalatable, tasteless
different	unlike, diverse, distinct, various	identical, same, similar, like, alike
dirty	filthy, grimy, soiled, dingy, unsanitary, polluted, grubby	clean, unsoiled, stainless, unstained, washed, cleansed
dishonest	lying, untruthful, untrustworthy, deceitful, crooked, devious, mendacious	honest, truthful, upright, virtuous, just, moral, fair

	Synonyms	Antonyms
eager	enthusiastic, keen, avid, fervent, ardent, zealous	indifferent, apathetic, uninterested, detached, impassive, unresponsive
easy	effortless, simple, uncomplicated	hard, difficult, complicated, complex, intricate, convoluted, tangled, perplexing
empty	vacant, hollow, unoccupied, uninhabited, barren	full, occupied, inhabited
enough	ample, sufficient, adequate, abundant, plenty	insufficient, inadequate
fair	just, impartial, equal, unbiased, evenhanded, equitable, objective	unfair, unjust, partial, discriminatory, biased, inequitable
faithful	loyal, true, devoted, steadfast, unwavering, constant, dependable, reliable, trustworthy, trusty	faithless, false, disloyal, treacherous, deceitful, perfidious, subversive, traitorous
fake	phony, false, artificial, imitation, bogus, counterfeit, pretended, feigned	real, actual, genuine, authentic, factual, unfeigned

	Synonyms	Antonyms
famous	noted, prominent, eminent, celebrated, illustrious, notorious	unknown, obscure, undistinguished, unfamiliar
far	distant, remote, faraway, outlying	near, close, adjacent, neighboring, adjoining
fast	rapid, quick, swift, speedy, fleet, expeditious	slow, unhurried, gradual, leisurely
foolish	ridiculous, silly, absurd, senseless, inane, asinine, witless, fatuous	clever, intelligent, brilliant, astute, serious, rational, logical, reasonable, sound, sensible
full	packed, loaded, filled, crowded, stuffed	empty, void, vacant, barren, bare, vacuous, unoccupied
funny	amusing, humorous, witty, hilarious, comical, ridiculous, jocular, whimsical	sad, serious, sober, somber, doleful, mournful, lugubrious
gentle	mild, soft, tender, kind, sensitive	harsh, rough, stern, loud, violent
good	fine, excellent, great, worthy, outstanding, admirable, respectable, splendid, superb, superior	bad, inferior, defective, poor, faulty, inadequate, shabby, mediocre, shoddy

	Synonyms	Antonyms
grand	magnificent, stately, majestic, splendid, impressive, dignified, palatial	ignoble, menial, low, mean, inferior, modest
grateful	thankful, pleased, appreciative, indebted, obliged, beholden	displeased, ungrateful, dissatisfied, discontented
great	wonderful, amazing, terrific, superb, remarkable, splendid, marvelous, sensational, fabulous, spectacular, phenomenal	terrible, awful, appalling dreadful, horrible, disgusting
heavy	weighty, ponderous, massive, hefty	light, weightless, buoyant
high	tall, lofty, towering, elevated	low, short, diminutive
hot	sweltering, sultry, torrid, warm, lukewarm, tepid	cold, chilly, icy, frigid, frosty, freezing
important	significant, substantial, consequential, crucial, critical, momentous, eventful, principal, chief, major, main	unimportant, minor, trivial, trifling, paltry, insignificant, slight, inconsequential, petty

	Synonyms	Antonyms
jealous	envious, resentful, grudging, covetous, green-eyed	content, satisfied, pleased
lively	active, energetic, vigorous, animated, inexhaustible	inactive, idle, inert
lonely	lonesome, homesick, alone, desolate, forlorn, isolated	cheerful, happy, jovial, joyous, delighted
long	lengthy, extensive, drawn-out, extended, protracted	short, brief, succinct, concise, condensed
loud	noisy, deafening, clamorous, blatant, clangorous, riotous, earsplitting	quiet, silent, still, noiseless, soundless, hushed, muffled
many	numerous, various, countless, innumerable, diverse, multitudinous	few, not many, scant
mean	cruel, malicious, disagreeable, contemptible, despicable, ignominious, shameful	nice, likable, kind, pleasant, friendly, agreeable, benevolent, lovable, personable
naked	nude, bare, unclothed, undressed	dressed, clothed, outfitted, costumed

	Synonyms	Antonyms
neat	tidy, trim, orderly, groomed, clean, ordered, natty, dapper	messy, dirty, slovenly, untidy, rumpled, slipshod, disheveled, disorderly
necessary	needed, essential, indispensable, important, urgent, crucial	unnecessary, needless, unessential, superfluous, unimportant
nervous	restless, fidgety, edgy, uptight, apprehensive, tense, excitable, high-strung	calm, peaceful, tranquil, unruffled, composed, pacific
old	elderly, aged, ancient, antique, antiquated, antediluvian	new, fresh, original, recent, novel, brand-new, youthful, callow, immature, juvenile
perfect	flawless, faultless, ideal, impeccable, matchless	imperfect, damaged, flawed, marred, defective, faulty, inadequate, deficient
plain	simple, modest, unadorned, uncomplicated, unpretentious	fancy, decorated, elaborate, ornate, embellished, elegant, luxurious
polite	courteous, well-mannered, gracious, civil, mannerly, considerate, respectful	impolite, insolent, discourteous, sassy, impertinent, brusque, impudent, uncivil, disrespectful, boorish

	Synonyms	Antonyms
pretty	beautiful, lovely, handsome, gorgeous, attractive, exquisite, comely, fair, pleasing, stunning	ugly, unattractive, unsightly hideous, homely, uncomely, monstrous
ready	prepared, set, fit, fitted, ripe, equipped, available, qualified	unprepared, unfit, unequipped, unqualified
rich	wealthy, affluent, prosperous, well-to-do, loaded, moneyed, well-off	poor, broke, indigent, needy, insolvent, destitute, hard up, penniless
rough	coarse, uneven, rugged, bumpy, craggy, jagged	smooth, even, level, flat plane
sad	unhappy, miserable, gloomy, depressed, melancholy, blue, downhearted, morose, dejected, dispirited, despondent	happy, blissful, merry, delighted, cheerful, blithe, contented, gladdened, joyful, jubilant, elated, jovial
safe	secure, protected, snug, safeguarded, harmless, sheltered, shielded, preserved, defended	unsafe, unprotected, insecure

	Synonyms	Antonyms
shy	bashful, timid, meek, reserved, diffident, demure, reticent, retiring, humble, modest, sheepish	outgoing, extroverted, gregarious, sociable, bold, forward, brazen, obtrusive, daring
sick	ill, ailing, sickly, unwell, diseased, afflicted	well, healthy, hardy, robust, hale
smart	intelligent, clever, bright, wise, learned, adroit, brilliant, sharp, ingenious	stupid, unintelligent, asinine, senseless, dull-witted, mindless
sour	tart, bitter, rancid, acidic, tangy	sweet, bland, mellow, sugary, pleasant
strange	odd, peculiar, unusual, funny, weird, abnormal, bizarre, atypical	usual, normal, ordinary, natural, regular, common, customary, typical
strong	powerful, hardy, muscular, vigorous, mighty, herculean, hearty, brawny	weak, feeble, helpless, puny, delicate, fragile, flimsy
stubborn	obstinate, willful, headstrong, rigid, inflexible, intractable, bull-headed, contumacious	yielding, pliable, pliant, amenable, willing, acquiescent, compliant, adaptable, adjustable, malleable

	Synonyms	Antonyms
thin	slender, slim, lean, slight, skinny, gaunt, lank, scrawny, emaciated	fat, overweight, portly, obese, chubby, stocky, stout, plump, corpulent
tired	exhausted, weary, worn, worn out, sleepy, fatigued, haggard, enervated, drained, bushed, overworked, spent, wearied	alert, attentive, wakeful, vigilant, strong, hearty, robust, powerful
violent	vehement, intense, vicious, destructive, wild, brutal, barbarous, savage, fierce	quiet, calm, peaceful, genteel, civilized, polite, civil, composed, pacific
wet	moist, humid, clammy, dank, moistened, soaked, drenched, saturated, sodden, waterlogged, dripping	dry, arid, desiccated, drought-ridden, parched, dehydrated
wild	untamed, fierce, ferocious, savage, agitated, stormy, frenzied, turbulent, riotous, boisterous	calm, peaceful, serene, tranquil, placid, pacific, still, unruffled, composed
wrong	incorrect, false, untrue, mistaken, inaccurate, erroneous	correct, accurate, right, precise, true, exact, actual

EXTRA

Fifty Synonyms for *Very*

Probably the most overused word in English is "very." When some writers want to make an adjective stronger or more emphatic, they often put "very" in front of it.

On the very hot day, the very tall woman and the very small dog walked very quickly along the very long road.

There is nothing wrong with "very" unless it's overused. Once or twice in a story is OK. More than that is probably too much. In a thesaurus, you will find synonyms for the overworked "very." Here are 50 of them.

absolutely	exquisitely	mightily	severely
actually	extraordinarily	monstrously	singularly
acutely	extremely	notably	strikingly
amazingly	famously	particularly	surprisingly
assuredly	glaringly	perfectly	truly
astonishingly	immeasurably	pointedly	uncommonly
certainly	incalculably	positively	unconditionally
decidedly	incredibly	powerfully	unequivocally
desperately	infinitely	prominently	unusually
downright	intensely	quite	utterly
emphatically	markedly	really	verily
exceedingly	marvelously	remarkably	wonderfully
exceptionally			

chapter 8

Build a Vast, Vivid, and Voluminous Vocabulary

The smartest person who speaks English knows only a small fraction of the words in the language. So there are plenty of words that you don't know—yet. But there's a lot that you can do to build up your vocabulary. Here's a four-step plan that can help.

1. **Be a Word Explorer.** Just as Columbus, Magellan, and all those other explorers of old looked for new lands to discover, you should be on the lookout for new words. They're all over the place. You can't avoid them.

   You'll see them in books, magazines, and newspapers. You'll find them in ads. You'll hear them in movies, on television, and even in other people's conversations.

   So capture those new words. Circle them, underline them, highlight them, draw arrows pointing to them. If you hear a new word, try to write it down as soon as possible. If you're not sure of the spelling, do the best you can. You can fix it up later. Do anything you can so that you don't lose a new word just when you've discovered it.

2. **Be a Word Detective.** Just as Sherlock Holmes and other famous detectives of long ago had to uncover facts, you have to be an investigator of words and figure them out, too.

   As soon as possible, look up your new word. It might be a good idea to have a paperback dictionary near your bed if you read before going to sleep. Some people carry electronic dictionaries in their book bags.

   Make sure that you understand the definition of the word. Refer back to the sentence that you saw it in. Try to find a meaning that fits that context. If there are words in the definition that you don't understand, look them up, too.

3. **Be a Flash-Card Maker.** One of the best learning tools in the world is one of the oldest and cheapest: flash cards. They need no electricity or connection to the Internet. They're silent, lightweight, and fit in your pocket. You can take them anywhere and use them anytime.

   Get a pack of 100 3-x-5-inch index cards at any stationery store. Cut them in half. That way you get 200 cards for the price of 100. That's a bargain.

   Write the vocabulary word on one side of the card. Flip the card over and write a clear definition on the other side. Put the part of speech down, too. If the word is a member of a word family (see Chapter 4 on page 93), you might want to put the word's relatives on the card to keep the family together. Some dictionaries give synonyms and antonyms (see Chapter 7 on page 117). You can add those to the back of your card, too, if you like.

   Making flash cards takes a little time, but it's time well spent. You are creating a wonderful study tool that you can use to learn and review vocabulary words for years to come.

   After your cards are made, use them. Pick up a card. Look at the word. Say the definition to yourself. Turn the card over. Did you get it right? When you've gone through all your cards, go over the ones you didn't know the first time. When you know them all, you're done.

   Keep adding to your flash cards. Pretty soon, you'll probably have hundreds of them. Review your cards often.

4. **Be a Word User.** Want to know the absolutely best way to make a new word yours? Use it! Soon after you've learned a new word, find a way to use it. Not all new words fit into everyday conversations easily, so if you can't slip the word in when you're talking to your friends, try to find a clever

way to use it in a report for school. Your teacher will be impressed. Use your new words when talking to adults. Try them out in e-mails to your friends. Use 'em or lose 'em.

The more you use a word that was once new, the more it will become part of your own vocabulary. The next time you see it in someone else's writing, you'll know what it means.

Many people have already used this plan to build up their vocabularies, and it really works. Now it's your turn. Put your explorer's hat on and go out and find those words!

Play Flash!, the vocabulary flash-card game, with one or two of your friends.

EXTRA

One player picks up a vocabulary flash card and says the word. Another player has to give the correct definition. If he or she can't think of the definition, the player with the card can give hints. If a correct definition is given, the person holding the card shouts, "Flash!"

If there are three players, one person says the word and the other two have to call out the correct meaning. The player holding the flash card gets to decide who said the correct definition first by shouting "Flash!" and pointing to the person who won that round.

Keep score. You can figure out your own system. For instance, getting the definition right in five seconds without help is worth five points. Deduct points if it takes longer than five seconds or if the player needs hints. Deduct two points if the wrong answer is given. Deduct one point for no answer. Keep score and switch sides after every word. The player with the most points wins, and the prize is a great vocabulary.

chapter 9

Vocabulary-Building Games

You might think that building up your vocabulary can sometimes be a chore, so here are six games to play with your friends to make it more fun to learn new words and improve your dictionary skills. You'll need at least one good, advanced (maybe even college-level) dictionary to get all the answers right. Remember, dictionaries word their definitions differently, so you many want to keep two or more dictionaries handy or use one of the on-line dictionaries on page 116. Good luck!

The "Hats and Plants" Eponym Game

Eponyms are people and places that became words. (See Chapter 1 on page 1.) Here are the names of four kinds of hats and nine plants that all came from eponyms. Use a good dictionary to see if you can discover the names of the people and places that gave us these words. Divide up the words with your friends and give points to the person who finds the answers in the shortest time. Answers are on pages 148–150.

Hats

Take a walk in any crowded city and you'll see plenty of eponyms—on people's heads!

derby   Stetson   homburg   fedora

Plants

Take a stroll in any garden and you'll see eponyms growing all around. Some of these people lived hundreds of years ago, but their names are still in bloom.

begonia	gardenia	sequoia
forsythia	magnolia	wisteria
fuchsia	poinsettia	zinnia

The "Where in the World?" Game

English has words from at least 100 different languages. Here is a suitcase full of words that came from foreign tongues. You might know what some of them mean. But what languages do they come from?

Two players can take turns in this game. The first one reads a word on the list and tries to guess what language it comes from. The player then looks the word up in a dictionary that gives etymologies (word origins). The player gets five points if he or she has guessed right. (Note: Your dictionary may tell you that a word came from more than one language, so if you guess any of the languages, you get your points.) Take turns and keep score. The answers are on pages 151–152 and in your dictionary. When you've done all the words on this list, continue playing the game by finding more words from foreign languages in a dictionary.

adobe	chocolate	khaki
algebra	chutney	Massachusetts
banana	clarinet	noodle
barbecue	coffee	opera
boomerang	dollar	orange
boss	frontier	pentagon
buccaneer	inch	ranch
bungalow	jar	satay
café	javelin	school
canyon	kangaroo	sky

spaghetti	tutti-frutti	yam
taco	voodoo	yoga
tea	waffle	zero

The "-ible or -able" Game

Below are a bunch of common words. If you put the prefix **in-** at the beginning of each one and either **-ible** or **-able** at the end of each one, you will create a word that means "not able to be" + the meaning of the base word.

For example, take **approach**, add the prefix **in-** and the suffix **-able** and you have the word **inapproachable**, which means "not able to be approached," as in the sentence, "When my science teacher is in a bad mood, he's inapproachable."

But here's the challenge. Some of the new words will end with **-ible** and some with **-able** and there's no rule or trick to help you know which. So plunk **in-** in front of one of these words, and choose either **-ible** or **-able** for the end. Then look your new word up in a dictionary. If you spelled it right, give yourself five points. Take turns with a friend.

Before you add **-ible** or **-able**, drop all silent *e*'s and the letters *-ate* at the ends of words. All other spelling changes are shown in parentheses.

Add **in-** to the front and **-ible** or **-able** to the end of these words. Answers are on page 153.

access	combust	control (controll)
admit (admiss)	comprehend	controvert
alter	(comprehens)	convert
appreciate	compress	convince
capacity (cap)	conceive	corrupt
coerce	condense	cure

decipher	estimate	separate
defect	excuse	suffer
defend (defens)	exhaust	support
define	express	suppress
destruct	extend (extens)	surmount
digest	extinguish	suscept
dispense	flex	tolerate
dispute	imitate	vary (vari)
distinguish	numerate	violate
divide (divis)	operate	
dominate (domit)	satiate	

The "Find the Right Store" Game

Pretend that you are in the biggest mall in the world. All your relatives have told you what they want for their birthdays. Your job is to go to the right store for each gift. First, you'd better go to a bookstore and get a good dictionary, because your relatives have asked for some weird things. Have fun on your shopping spree!

Match the gift to the store. Give yourself five points for every store you guess correctly. Take turns with a friend. Answers are on pages 153–154.

You can buy this gift	in what kind of store?
anthology	plants
armoire	art supplies
beret	kitchenware
brooch	music
carburetor	hardware
chronometer	jewelry

You can buy this gift	in what kind of store?
dieffenbachia	pets
duvet	shoes
ferret	hats
fly rod	furniture
libretto	auto supply
oxfords	food
pigments	sporting goods
quiche	home electronics
router	watches
scanner	luggage
weekender	computers
wok	bedding
woofer	books

The "Get the Animals Home" Game

Animals live in many different places, on (and sometimes under) the land, in the air, under the water, etc. All the animals below are lost. Use your dictionary and help them find their way home. Birds belong **in the air**, fish **under the sea**, and land animals **on the land**. Give yourself five points for every animal you place in its natural environment. Take turns with a friend. Answers are on page 154.

betta	eland	gourami
blenny	finch	grouper
chickadee	gazelle	hamadryas
Chihuahua	gecko	harrier
chinchilla	gibbon	hedgehog
cockatoo	goby	hyena

iguana	piranha	swordtail
kookaburra	platy	tetra
macaw	puffer	thrasher
molly	sapsucker	touraco
mudskipper	shrike	towhee
muntjac	siamang	vulture
nutcracker	sika	warbler
ocelot	stingray	wrasse

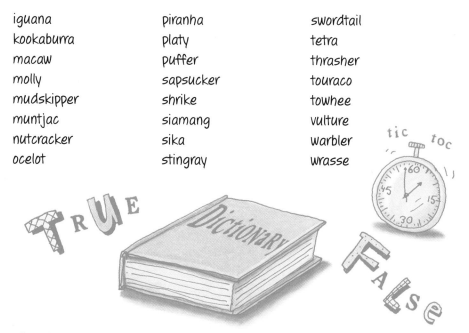

The "True or False?" Game

Here's a game for you and your friends to make up yourselves. Flip through a good dictionary and find a new, strange, or weird word or a word with a peculiar or amazing definition. Make up one true or false question about that word.

For instance, suppose you found **humus** (pronounced "HYOO•muhss"). You could say to your friend, "Humus helps plants grow. True or false?" Or, "Humus would taste great as an ice cream topping. True or false?"

If your friend can't decide, he or she can have one minute to look up the word in a dictionary and say "True" or "False." Award 10 points for a right answer without having to use a dictionary, 5 points for a right answer using a dictionary.

Since humus is dark, rich soil formed from rotting plants and decayed animals, and helps plants grow, the answer to the first question would be *true*, and the answer to the second question would definitely be *false*!

Take turns and keep score to see who gets the most questions right.

Answers

Answers to the "Hats and Plants" Eponym Game

Hats

derby: Edward Stanley, the Earl of Derby, established a famous horse race called the Derby in England in 1780. Americans liked the stiff, dome-shape, felt hats they saw British men wearing to the race. They brought samples back home, and a hatmaker advertised them as the Derby hats. Soon the popular hat was called just a derby.

Stetson: In the 1860s, John Stetson took a trip west for his health. He got an idea for a cowboy hat and starting making it back in Philadelphia. He sold millions of them. Ever since, the wide-brimmed, high-crowned felt hat has been called a Stetson.

homburg: This man's felt hat with a soft, dented crown and a slightly rolled brim was first manufactured in the German city of Homburg.

fedora: A fedora is a soft felt hat with a low crown creased lengthwise and a brim that can be turned up or down. It was named after Fedora, the heroine of an 1882 French play. Fedora wore a hat in the play that was later restyled and became popular with men.

Plants

begonia: Michel Bégon had a great job working for the king of France as the governor of a Caribbean island in the 1600s. He loved studying the flora of the island, and this plant with brightly colored leaves (which was actually discovered by a botanist-monk in Mexico) was named after him.

forsythia: This shrub with many lovely yellow flowers originally came from China. Samples of it were brought back to England in the 1700s, and it was named in honor of William Forsyth, a Scottish horticulturist, famous British gardener, and head of the Royal Gardens in London.

fuchsia: Leonhard Fuchs, a famous German doctor and professor in the 1500s, made flowers into medicine to treat sick people. He wrote an important book about medicinal plants. A South American shrub with drooping purplish-red flowers was named fuchsia in honor of this pioneering doctor.

gardenia: A Scottish-born American doctor-botanist, Alexander Garden, moved to London after the Revolutionary War. For his loyal support of England, the English named the gardenia, a shrub with glossy evergreen leaves and fragrant white flowers, after Dr. Garden.

magnolia: In the 1600s, French doctor Pierre Magnol wrote a famous book about tree families. In his honor a tree family was named magnolia. These shrubs and trees have huge, showy flowers and can grow up to 100 feet high. Mississippi likes the plant so much it calls itself the Magnolia State.

poinsettia: At Christmas you see a holiday plant with large, bright red flowers. It was named after Joel Poinsett, a rich medical school dropout from South Carolina. The president of the United States appointed him the first minister to Mexico in 1825. Poinsett brought home a strange Mexican plant and cultivated it. Later it was named poinsettia after him.

sequoia: There was no Native American written language until the 1800s. Sequoyah (also known as George Gist), a Cherokee, recognized the need for a Cherokee writing system. He spent 12 years creating the Cherokee alphabet, "Talking Leaves." It is made up of the 85 different sounds in the Cherokee language. This alphabet made it possible for Cherokees to read and write in their own language. Sequoyah worked for his people as a statesperson and diplomat until he died in his 60s in 1843. No wonder the tallest and oldest living things on earth, the giant sequoia trees, are named for this great Native American.

wisteria: On some houses you might see climbing vines with drooping clusters of purplish or white flowers. That's wisteria, named for Casper Wistar, a Philadelphia doctor-professor. He wrote the first American book on anatomy, published in the early 1800s. People wanted to name a beautiful vine after him. It was supposed to be called wistaria but it was spelled wrong, and that's how it's been ever since.

zinnia: The state flower of Indiana is the zinnia, a garden plant with flowers of many different colors. It completes its entire life cycle in a single growing season and quickly dies with the first frost. Dr. Johann Zinn, a German botanist and physician of the 1700s, had a bright, brief life just like this flower. He wrote the first book on the anatomy of the eye, but he died at age 32, so the short-lived zinnia is a fitting tribute to him.

Answers to the "Where in the World?" Game

Note: If your dictionary gives more languages than those listed below, those languages count as right answers, too.

Word	Language
adobe	Spanish from Arabic
algebra	Middle English and Italian from Medieval Latin from Arabic
banana	Portuguese and Spanish from Wolof (an African language)
barbecue	Spanish from Taíno (a language of the Caribbean)
boomerang	Dharuk (Aboriginal language of southeast Australia)
boss	Dutch
buccaneer	French
bungalow	Hindi (a language of India)
café	French from Italian from Ottoman Turkish
canyon	Spanish from Latin from Greek
chocolate	Spanish from Nahuatl (a language of central Mexican Indians)
chutney	Hindi
clarinet	French from Latin
coffee	Turkish from Arabic
dollar	German
frontier	Middle English from Old French
inch	Middle English from Old English from Latin
jar	Middle English from Old French from Medieval Latin from Arabic

Word	Language
javelin	Middle English from Old French
kangaroo	Guugu Yimidhirr (Aboriginal language of northeast Australia)
khaki	Urdu (an Indian language used in Pakistan and India) from Persian from Middle Persian
Massachusetts	Algonquin
noodle	German
opera	Italian from Latin
orange	Middle English from Old French from Old Italian from Arabic from Persian
pentagon	Latin from Greek
ranch	Spanish from Old French
satay	Malay or Indonesian
school	Middle English from Old English from Latin from Greek
sky	Middle English from Old Norse
spaghetti	Italian
taco	Spanish
tea	Dutch from Malay from Chinese
tutti-frutti	Italian
voodoo	Louisiana French from Ewe (an African language)
waffle	Dutch
yam	Portuguese or Spanish from Mandingo (an African language)
yoga	Hindi from Sanskrit
zero	Italian from Medieval Latin from Arabic

Answers to the "-ible or -able" Game

inaccessible	incurable	inextensible
inadmissible	indecipherable	inextinguishable
inalterable	indefectible	inflexible
inappreciable	indefensible	inimitable
incapable	indefinable	innumerable
incoercible	indestructible	inoperable
incombustible	indigestible	insatiable
incomprehensible	indispensable	inseparable
incompressible	indisputable	insufferable
inconceivable	indistinguishable	insupportable
incondensable	indivisible	insuppressible
incontrollable	indomitable	insurmountable
incontrovertible	inestimable	insusceptible
inconvertible	inexcusable	intolerable
inconvincible	inexhaustible	invariable
incorruptible	inexpressible	inviolable

Answers to the "Find the Right Store" Game

Gift	Store
anthology	books
armoire	furniture
beret	hats
brooch	jewelry
carburetor	auto supply
chronometer	watches
dieffenbachia	plants
duvet	bedding
ferret	pets

Gift	Store
fly rod	sporting goods
libretto	music
oxfords	shoes
pigments	art supplies
quiche	food
router	hardware
scanner	computers
weekender	luggage
wok	kitchenware
woofer	home electronics

Answers to the "Get the Animals Home" Game

In the Air	In the Water	On the Land
chickadee	betta	Chihuahua
cockatoo	blenny	chinchilla
finch	goby	eland
harrier	gourami	gazelle
kookaburra	grouper	gecko
macaw	molly	gibbon
nutcracker	mudskipper	hamadryas
sapsucker	piranha	hedgehog
shrike	platy	hyena
thrasher	puffer	iguana
touraco	stingray	muntjac
towhee	swordtail	ocelot
vulture	tetra	siamang
warbler	wrasse	sika

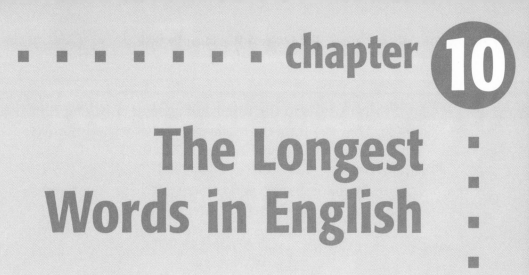

The Longest
Words in English

The shortest words in the English language are *a* and *I*, of course. They're pretty easy to learn, and everybody knows what they mean. (They're easy to spell, too.)

But many people love long words—really, really l-o-o-o-ng words. Even William Shakespeare liked an occasional word that went on and on. He used a 27-letter word—honorificabilitudinitatibus—in one of his plays, *Love's Labour's Lost*. (It means "with honorableness.") For some reason, it just didn't catch on with everyday folk.

In this chapter you'll find the four longest words in English. Impress your friends by dropping them into conversation one day, or slip one of them into an e-mail. Challenge yourself to learn how to spell them (but only if you have a lot of free time). And if you use one of these words in a paper for school, your teacher will be wowed.

antidisestablishmentarianism (28 letters)

Many people have heard of this word, but few know what it means. It's not easy to understand, so please pay attention. In the late 1800s, in England, some people believed that the government should withdraw its official support of religion. Other people, however, believed just the opposite. Those people believed in *antidisestablishmentarianism*, a doctrine that's against taking government support away from the church.

floccinaucinihilipipification (29 letters)

This old word from the 1700s means the action or habit of estimating something as being worthless. A person who says, "That broken-down old jalopy you call a car isn't worth two cents," is practicing *floccinaucinihilipipification*.

supercalifragilisticexpialidocious (34 letters)

This nonsense word was made up in 1964 for a song in the movie *Mary Poppins*. It means "very good" or "great" and is probably the best known long word in the world.

pneumonoultramicroscopicsilicovolcanoconiosis (45 letters)

This humongous word names a lung disease that coal miners can get if they breathe in too much very fine silicon dust. If you split the word up like this—*pneumono ultra microscopic silico volcano coniosis*—it starts to make a little more sense, doesn't it?

There is even one science word that's too immense to include in this book. It was printed out only once, in 1981, in a science magazine called *Nature*. It is approximately 207,000 letters long, and it means the nucleotide links that make up human mitochondrial DNA. Really.

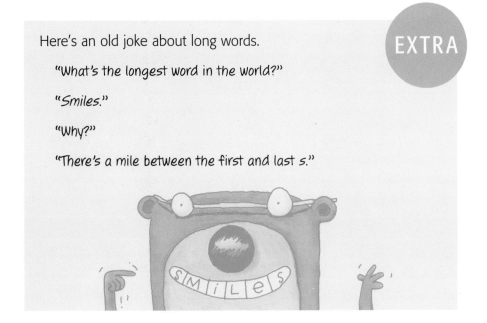

Here's an old joke about long words.

EXTRA

"What's the longest word in the world?"

"Smiles."

"Why?"

"There's a mile between the first and last s."

chapter **11**

How Words Change

The English language is always growing, and the meanings, spellings, and pronunciations of words change over time and from place to place. That's why dictionaries have to be updated frequently.

How Words Change Over Time

Read the following sentence. You'll understand every word.

"She is a cool girl who likes to have fun with her dog and then grab her mouse and get her e-mail."

But many years ago, people might have thought it meant

"No such word is a not-too-cold young male or female who likes to have not a word that's used with her specific kind of hound and then grab her small rodent and get her e-leather sack."

Huh? Some explanations are in order.

How many times a day do you say **she**? Surprisingly, there was no such word before the year A.D. 1000. The closest word was *heo*, which sounded very much like *he* and also meant *"they."* That must have been confusing. Finally people started using **she** to mean "a girl" or "a woman," and that helped clear up the confusion.

Cool has meant "not too hot or too cold" for centuries, but more recently it has taken on a slang meaning of "terrific, great, excellent."

You may be surprised to learn that in the Middle Ages **girl** meant both "a boy" or "a girl," and only years later did it come to refer only to young females.

People started using the word **fun** in the 1700s, but people who were really educated didn't use it at all. (They were probably so busy learning stuff, they didn't have much time for fun.)

Dogge was an English word from long ago that referred to a very specific breed of dogs that were large and powerful. *Hund* (or *hound*) was the word that meant dogs in general. Today **dog** is the general word, and **hound** refers mainly to hunting dogs. The words switched places—the specific became general and the general became specific.

Before the 1960s, a **mouse** was just a small rodent. Then it became the name of a handheld, button-controlled pointing device attached to your computer. Someone who didn't know that the word had a new meaning would be dumbfounded to think of people taking small rodents in their hands and rolling them on flat surfaces to operate computers.

Mail originally meant "a leather sack that carried letters and packages" (French word: *male*). Today it means "letters and packages," not the sack.

So we can see that over the course of many years, words can change their meanings or gain additional meanings.

How Words Change from Place to Place: Regionalisms and Dialects

Sometimes people in one place use words and expressions that don't exist elsewhere. Sometimes people pronounce words differently in different geographic locations. Some dictionaries will point out regional words and special dialects (pronunciations). Today people move easily from place to place, and they take their regional words and phrases with them. Television shows and movies also help to spread regionalisms around the country. Here are some examples.

Suppose, on a hot day, you want a carbonated soft drink. If you're in the Midwest or westward, ask for a pop. If you're in the northeastern states, order a soda. If you're anywhere near or in Boston, call it a tonic. If you're in the South, just cold drink will do. *Whew!* All that just to cool off.

If on that same hot day, you want to take a dip in a little stream of water, be careful how you ask for directions to the nearest creek. In some parts of the country, the word rhymes with *sneak*. In other parts, it rhymes with *trick*. In some places, people pronounce it both ways.

If you're visiting your grandmother, and you'd like to cook yourself eggs, ask Grandma for her skillet in some states between the North and South (especially the upper South); her spider in New England and along the coasts of New Jersey, Virginia, and North and South Carolina; and her plain old frying pan in other regions.

Call your aunt "ant" or "ahnt," depending on where you live, who raised you, and how your family pronounces the word.

If you want to make a wish after eating a chicken or turkey, you'll pull apart a wishbone in the northern United States, a pully-bone or pull-bone in the southern states, and a lucky-bone in northern New England and eastern Virginia.

Tomato is pronounced "tuh-MAY-toe" in most places, but "tuh-MAH-toe" in other locales (like eastern Virginia and New England).

If you feel a raindrop while you're in bed, ask someone to please fix your "roof" or your "ruf," depending on where you live in this country. Both pronunciations are spelled roof.

If you want to take a bath, you turn on the faucet, spigot, or tap, depending on where in the United States your bathtub is.

Informal vs. Formal Language

All of us have different sets of vocabularies. There are the words and phrases we use when we talk to our friends. But we change the way we express ourselves when we write a report for school. Some people call these "interpersonal" and "academic" vocabularies. One is informal and easygoing, and the other follows stricter rules of vocabulary and grammar. Here are examples.

Informal (talking on the phone to a friend):

I got this great CD by a rock band called Vision of Disorder. It's heavy metal and it's amazing. There are these five guys, but my friend Jen—you know, the one with the tattoos—she thinks the singer, Tim, is like so cool. The music is right in your face with the drums and the guitars and the screaming. My mom calls it like noise. But it's amazing!

Formal (research report for school):

Wolfgang Amadeus Mozart was born in Salzburg, Austria, in 1754. He is considered by most musical historians to be one of the greatest and most prolific composers in history. Mozart demonstrated his musical genius when very young. He began composing at age five and giving piano concerts before royalty at six. At seven, he toured London and Paris and astonished his listeners with his precocious talents.

Slang Expressions

Slang is a kind of language that you use mostly in casual and playful speech. Slang words and phrases are not always thought of as good English, and you wouldn't use much slang if you had to make a serious speech or write a paper for school. Some slang doesn't last very long, but it can be colorful, vivid, and expressive when it's being used. Some of this language does catch on, and if it's in your dictionary, it will be identified as slang.

Slang can come from politics, news events, entertainment, business and finance, computers, technology, crime stories, science fiction, sports, etc. Here are some slang words and expressions that were popular in recent years, but they may be replaced with new sayings in the future.

> **A-OK** the very best
> **belly-up** out of business; bankrupt
> **boondoggle** a program that wastes taxpayers' money
> **chop shop** place where stolen cars are taken apart so that their parts can be sold separately
> **Cinderella team** a sports team with little hope of success at the beginning of a season and then wins big at the end
> **cybrarian** librarian who uses the Internet at work
> **spin doctor** (or spin master) a public relations person who slants a potentially damaging news story to make it seem more favorable for someone
> **talking heads** analysts who talk on television

Avoiding Sexist Language

At one time, certain jobs were thought of as being men's jobs or women's jobs, and names were given to those jobs that often ended with -*man* or -*ess*. Some people think those job titles are sexist and show stereotyping or even discrimination based on gender, especially against women.

Today anybody can hold any job, so we try to use names that can relate to both men and women.

Old Names (considered by some people to be sexist)	New Names (gender-free)
actor and actress	actor
anchorman and anchorwoman	anchor
aviator and aviatrix	aviator, pilot
chairman	chair or chairperson
congressman	congressperson
fireman	firefighter
mailman	mail carrier
policeman	police officer
steward and stewardess	flight attendant
waiter and waitress	server

Compound Words

Common compound words are written without a space (*beanbag*), with a space (*lawn mower*), or with a hyphen (*hard-boiled*).

New compounds can change over time. For example, when the first small, boxlike passenger van came out, it was called a mini van. As this vehicle became more popular, the two words were joined by a hyphen to become mini-van. Today, it's a one-word compound, minivan.

The same journey from open compound (two words) to hypenated compound to closed compound (one word) is being taken today by Web site, Web-site, and Website.

Hungry? How would you like a delicious long sandwich **EXTRA** filled with layers of meats and cheeses on a French bread or a crusty Italian roll? A lot of people would call that a submarine sandwich or a sub. But imagine you're taking a trip across America from North to South, East to West. That very same sandwich would be called by all these names:

Italian sandwich in Maine

grinder in California and New England

hero in New York City

hoagie in the Delaware Valley (Philadelphia and southern New Jersey)

Cuban sandwich in Miami

poor boy along the Gulf (of Mexico) Coast states of the southern United States

chapter 12

One Hundred Great Words

H ere are 100 terrific words to know. Remember, some word specialists think there could be as many as a million words in English. If you learn these 100, you'll have only 999,900 more to go! Better get started.

These are the abbreviations for the parts of speech:

n. = noun
adj. = adjective
v. = verb

abundant (uh•BUN•dunt) *adj.* Present in large quantities; plentiful or bountiful (amount of something).

Mrs. Penn has an abundant supply of knickknacks and bric-a-bracs.

accelerate (ak•SEL•uh•rayt) *v.* To move or cause to move faster and faster; to speed up.

If the roller coaster accelerates, Sybil will get dizzy.

allege (uh•LEJ) *v.* To state something is positively true; to accuse a person of doing something wrong without showing proof.

Peaches alleged that Tiger had spilled the milk.

arrogant (ar•uh•GUNT) *adj.* Having too high an opinion of yourself; showing self-importance and disregard for others.

That arrogant kid thought he was the greatest actor in the world.

bias (BYE•us) *n.* An unfair like or dislike of someone or something; prejudice, partiality, unfairness.

In Human Issues class, we learned to recognize and avoid bias against people.

boisterous (BOY•stur•us) *adj.* Full of noisy enthusiasm and energy; energetic, unruly, rowdy.

Jade was being so boisterous that Cindy couldn't do her homework.

calamity (kuh•LAM•i•tee) *n.* A terrible disaster or catastrophe.

It was a calamity for the town when the hurricane struck.

chaos (KAY•os) *n.* A state of total disorder and confusion; bedlam, pandemonium, mayhem.

There's never any chaos in Ms. Youngman's class because the students gladly obey her.

cherish (CHAYR•ish) *v.* To feel great love for someone or something.

Dr. Sen cherishes his children and always writes poems to them.

compassion (kum•PASH•un) *n.* A feeling of sympathy for someone who is suffering and a desire to help relieve the pain.

Harriet always feels great compassion for those who are needy.

compatible (kum•PAT•uh•bul) *adj.* Able to live, work, or be used together without difficulty; well-matched, well-suited.

Do you think a green polka-dotted sofa is compatible with orange-striped wallpaper?

confound (kun•FOUND) *v.* To puzzle, perplex, or confuse someone and make him or her uncertain of something; to bewilder or mystify.

Math confounds many kids, but Mrs. Scotto, the math teacher, clears everything up nicely.

consensus (kun•SEN•sus) *n.* A general agreement among the members of a group.

The consensus of the class was that the homework was actually fun.

consume (kun•SOOM) *v.* To use something up; to eat or drink something.

We must try to conserve, not consume, our natural resources.

crucial (KROO•shul) *adj.* Extremely important, significant, critical, and essential; vital.

It was crucial for David to fix his computer so that he could finish his work by the deadline.

culprit (KUL•prit) *n.* A person who is guilty of a crime; wrongdoer.

The principal thinks she knows the identity of the culprit who did the damage.

defy (di•FYE) *v.* To stand up to someone and refuse to obey; to confront and challenge someone.

My pet rabbit always defies my orders when I tell her to go to her cage.

desolate (DES•uh•lit) *adj.* Deserted, isolated, lonely.

The old, abandoned farmhouse looked desolate.

deteriorate (di•TIR•ee•uh•rayt) *v.* To make or become worse; decline, depreciate.

My house deteriorated in value after the lightning bolt struck it.

devastate (dev•uh•STAYT) *v.* To damage something badly; to destroy; to upset someone terribly.

The tornado devastated the playground, but we'll rebuild it.

distort (di•STORT) *v.* To twist out of shape; to change the facts in a way that is misleading.

The reporter distorted the news and made it seem worse than it was.

dynamic (dye•NAM•ik) *adj.* Energetic, enthusiastic, and very good at getting things done; vibrant, forceful.

Aaron is a dynamic young man and should go very far in life.

ecstasy (EK•stuh•see) *n.* A feeling of tremendous happiness.

When Rajeev hit the home run, ecstasy filled him from head to toe.

eloquent (EL•uh•kwunt) *adj*. Expressed clearly, forceful-ly, and persuasively; fluent, articulate, expressive.

Neena made an eloquent speech about the need for fun in life.

emphatic (em•FAT•ik) *adj*. Done with emphasis; force-ful and definite; vigorous and firm.

Ms. Kilmer was emphatic when she told the students that there was no gum chewing allowed.

enhance (en•HANS) *v*. To make something better, greater, more beautiful, or more valuable.

The dentist said that the braces on Assaf's teeth would someday enhance his smile.

evade (i•VAYD) *v*. To avoid somebody or escape doing something unpleasant (sometimes by trickery).

Stanley was a master at evading punishment for his mischief.

exasperate (ig•ZAS•puh•rayt) *v*. To make a person very angry, impatient, or frustrated.

Mango and Cocoa sometimes exasperate the neighbors with their barking.

fluctuate (FLUK•choo•ayt) *v*. To shift back and forth or up and down; to change irregularly.

Tamika's spelling test grades fluctuated from 66 to 100.

fluent (FLOO•unt) *adj*. Able to express yourself effortlessly and correctly; articulate, eloquent, voluble.

Monica has traveled widely and is fluent in many languages.

foliage (FOH•lee•ij) *n*. The leaves of plants and trees.

The colorful fall foliage in Vermont is breathtakingly gorgeous.

formidable (FOR•mi•duh•bul) *adj*. Hard to deal with or overcome; fearsome; causing dread.

Watch out for Justin; he's a formidable football player.

frivolous (FRIV•uh•lus) *adj*. Not worth serious attention; silly, trivial, not important, inconsequential.

This is an extremely serious matter, not a time for frivolous behavior!

futile (FYOO•tul or FYOO•tile) *adj*. Useless, unsuccessful, ineffective, pointless, a waste of time.

It was futile for Shana to try to teach Sasha anything useful.

grapple (GRAP•ul) *v*. To grab hold of and wrestle with a person; to struggle with a difficult problem and try to solve it.

Mrs. Potter, the seventh grade dean, was grappling with the scheduling problems.

haphazard (hap•HAZ•urd) *adj.* Disorganized, un-planned, careless, and by chance.

Dr. Soghoian planned everything in advance and never did things haphazardly.

hesitant (HEZ•uh•tunt) *adj.* Unsure and not confident about how to act; acting in an uncertain manner.

Jessica was never hesitant about driving her new car in the snowstorm.

hinder (HIN•der) *v.* To make things difficult for some-one; to get in the way of; to block the progress of a person or thing.

Darling Amanda always tries to help, never hinder, people.

impetuous (im•PECH•oo•us) *adj.* Done without thought; impulsive, rash, hasty, spontaneous.

Impetuously, Kurt asked Bonnie to marry him, and she screamed, "Yes!"

indignant (in•DIG•nunt) *adj.* Upset, angry, or annoyed at a perceived injustice; offended, resentful.

Tim was never indignant if anyone said his music was too loud.

industrious (in•DUS•tree•us) *adj.* Steadily hardwork-ing, conscientious, energetic, and diligent.

Jen is an industrious jewelry designer who makes fan-tastic bracelets, necklaces, and rings.

insolent (IN•suh•lunt) *adj.* Disrespectful, rude, insulting, and outspoken in speech or behavior.

It really was insolent of Latoya to say Sharonda's new hairdo looked liked she'd been hit by a cyclone..

instigate (IN•stuh•gayt) *v.* To get something started; to cause trouble by urging someone to do something wrong.

If Howard tries to instigate any trouble, tell him to stop.

intercept (in•tur•SEPT) *v.* To block the movement of people or things by stopping, seizing, interrupting, or deflecting them.

The police intercepted the peanut butter thieves as they tried to escape from town.

irate (EYE•rayt *or* eye•RAYT) *adj.* Extremely angry; enraged, furious, incensed.

Harry was irate when Norma dared to correct his spelling.

lenient (LEEN•yunt *or* LEE•nee•unt) *adj.* Not harsh or strict; tolerant and permissive; flexible where rules are concerned.

Ashley wishes that Dennis would be a more lenient father, but Lynda thinks he's just fine.

longevity (long•JEV•i•tee) *n.* Long life; great duration of life; greatly extended existence.

Did you see the advertisement for the battery you never have to replace because of its longevity?

mediocre (me•dee•OH•KUR) *adj.* Not great or terrible; of average quality; ordinary, common.

The movie wasn't just mediocre; it was horrible!

melancholy (MEL•un•*kol*•ee) *adj.* Feeling a gentle sadness or thoughtful unhappiness.

Helene is always upbeat and peppy and never, ever melancholy.

momentous (moh•MEN•tus) *adj.* Very important and significant; extremely meaningful.

Winning the award was a momentous occasion for Ellen.

nimble (NIM•bul) *adj.* Moving quickly and lightly; agile.

After a good night's sleep, Joseph is very nimble when he jumps out of bed.

nonchalant (non•shuh•LAWNT) *adj.* Calmly unconcerned about things; cool, even-tempered, composed, and unruffled.

Was Ms. Freedman excited or nonchalant when her class won the top science fair prize?

nostalgia (nos•TAL•juh) *n.* A feeling of sadness, happiness, and bittersweet longing for people or things in the past.

Nostalgia comes over Fran when she thinks about her childhood in Chicago.

obscure (ob•SKYOOR) *adj.* Not well known; hard to understand because something is not clearly expressed.

He is an obscure author today because many readers found what he wrote very obscure.

obsolete (ob•suh•LEET *or* OB•suh•leet) *adj.* No longer used; out-of-date; outmoded and replaced by something newer.

Miriam writes with a quill pen, which many people think is an obsolete writing instrument.

obstacle (OB•stuh•kul) *n.* A person or thing that gets in your way and blocks your progress; obstruction, impediment.

Sandra never lets any obstacle get in her way, no matter how great.

optimist (OP•tuh•mist) *n.* A person who believes things will work out for the best; a positive person.

What an optimist Peter is! He thinks the rain will stop in time for the parade.

perishable (PER•ish•uh•bul) *adj.* Likely to decay, rot, or spoil quickly.

Put the butter in the refrigerator; it's perishable.

persistent (pur•SIS•tunt) *adj.* Refusing to give up; continuing steadily despite problems; lasting.

Lorrie was always persistent in her attempts to help all students.

phenomenon (fi•NOM•uh•non) *n.* Something remarkable, marvelous, or highly unusual.

The aurora borealis in Alaska is one of nature's most awesome phenomena.

predicament (pri•DIK•uh•munt) *n.* A very difficult, awkward, embarrassing, or unpleasant situation with no easy solution; dilemma, mess, "pickle."

Helen was in a predicament when her dress ripped just as she was about to go onstage.

presume (pri•ZOOM) *v.* To suppose that a thing is true without having all the facts to prove it.

Laurie presumed that Glenn had the gerbil food in his pocket, but he thought she did.

prosper (PROS•pur) *v.* To make a lot of money through hard word or good luck; to thrive, flourish.

John prospered in the satellite telephone business.

protrude (proh•TROOD) *v.* To stick out; to project or push outward.

Steve, the architect, had to redraw the plans because the building was protruding into the lake.

provoke (pruh•VOKE) *v.* To annoy a person and make him or her angry, annoyed, or resentful; to cause or bring on.

Arnold is careful never to provoke Arlene because the consequences might be severe.

prudent (PROOD•nt) *adj.* Wise, sensible, and practical in everyday matters; using good judgment; cautious and careful.

Mr. Barnes is a prudent man and never wastes his money.

punctual (PUNGK•choo•ul) *adj.* Right on time; prompt, without delay.

Jane is punctual and never arrives even one minute late to an appointment.

radiant (RAY•dee•unt) *adj.* Shining with a bright or glowing light; showing energy, joy, or good health.

After her vacation on a tropical island, Karen was well rested and radiant.

recuperate (ri•KOO•puh•*rayt*) *v.* To get your health and strength back after a sickness or injury; to recover.

After Barbara recuperated from her knee surgery, she was out nightly, dancing wildly.

relinquish (ri•LING•kwish) *v.* To give up something; to let go of something; to surrender something.

The dog didn't want to relinquish his favorite rubber bone.

reluctant (ri•LUK•tunt) *adj.* Not wanting to do something; feeling unwillingness; having no enthusiasm to do something.

Shelley was reluctant to let her students cover one another from head to foot with clay.

repulsive (ri•PUHL•siv) *adj.* Extremely disgusting, loathsome, revolting, distasteful, and offensive.

I cover my eyes whenever there's something repulsive in a movie.

revenue (REV•uh•*noo* or REV•uh•*nyoo*) *n.* The money a government collects from taxes and other sources; the income a business or investment makes.

Business is good, revenue is up, and the company president is happy.

rivalry (RYE•vul•ree) *n.* Competition between two parties; competitiveness; the act of competing.

There's always been a fierce rivalry between those two soccer teams.

ruthless (ROOTH•lis) *adj.* Very cruel and without any pity or mercy; callous, cold-blooded.

It took the whole movie for the superhero to finally defeat his ruthless opponent.

scrumptious (SKRUMP•shus) *adj.* Delicious, delectable.

I can't wait to eat one of Aunt Rozzie's scrumptious fruit-and-nut pies.

scrutinize (SKROO•tuhn•*ize*) *v.* To examine something closely; to inspect or study very carefully.

Judi scrutinizes every e-mail carefully to search for hidden meanings.

shrewd (SHROOD) *adj.* Keenly intelligent and clever in business, politics, etc.; smart, sharp, perceptive.

A lot of people seek Jerry's advice because he's a very shrewd person.

sluggish (SLUG•ish) *adj.* Moving or acting slowly and without energy; inactive.

Len felt very sluggish after walking the beat all day in the hot sun.

stamina (STAM•uh•nuh) *n.* Physical strength or mental energy to keep doing something for a long time.

It takes a lot of stamina for Lynette to arrange hundreds of flowers in that huge vase.

stifle (STYE•ful) *v.* To hold back or stop something from happening; to keep in; to interrupt or cut off.

Paula had to stifle several yawns while listening to the long, boring speech.

substantial (suhb•STAN•shul) *adj.* Big and solid; great in amount, importance, or value; strong, ample.

Loraine knows a substantial amount about teaching little kids.

synchronize (SING•kruh•*nyze*) *v.* To make things work together or happen at the same time or the same rate.

Sharmila synchronized her watch with the clock in the tower before she threw the switch.

taunt (TAWNT) *v.* To make a person angry and upset by provoking, ridiculing, or mocking him or her.

Don't ever taunt Nicola; she's small, but very tough.

temperament (TEM•pruh•munt) *n.* Your character, personality, or nature; the way you usually act, think, or respond to people and situations.

Fatima has a friendly temperament, so we always invite her to our parties.

tranquil (TRANG•kwul) *adj.* Peaceful, calm, and free of any disturbance; quiet, still, serene.

Out here in the woods, away from the noise of the big city, the night is amazingly tranquil.

tremor (TREM•ur) *n.* A trembling or quivering movement; a slight shaking or vibration (sometimes of the earth).

When Chandranath felt the tremor under his feet, he wondered if it was the subway or an earthquake.

undaunted (un•DAWN•tid) *adj.* Not frightened by danger; not afraid of defeat, failure, or loss; not discouraged; brave.

Kawano, the lion tamer, was undaunted by the gaping mouth of the huge, hungry cat.

unprecedented (un•PRESS•i•*den*•tid) *adj.* Never done or known of before; without any earlier example; first-time.

No one had ever climbed this mountain before in the wintertime; it was an unprecedented event.

unwieldy (uhn•WEEL•dee) *adj.* Hard to hold or handle because of its large size, awkward shape, or heavy weight.

The two movers had trouble carrying the unwieldy piano up the flights of narrow steps.

utensil (yoo•TEN•sul) *n.* A tool, instrument, or container used to do or make something.

A spatula is a very useful kitchen utensil.

valiant (VAL•yunt) *adj.* Very brave, courageous, dedicated, and steadfast; fearless, heroic, gallant.

Valerie was very valiant when she saved Val from the hidden valley on Valentine's Day.

veto (VEE•tow) *v.* To refuse to approve something; to prohibit or reject something; to stop a bill from becoming a law.

President Sortino will definitely veto this bill because she thinks it might hurt the environment.

vigorous (VIG•uh•rus) *adj.* Extremely strong, active, and energetic in body and mind; lively, robust.

Teddy Roosevelt was a frail child, but a very vigorous adult because he exercised and made himself strong.

wary (WAIR•ee) *adj.* Cautious, watchful; on guard.

Detective Rivera was always wary when she arrived at the scene of a crime.

wholesome (HOLE•sum) *adj.* Good for your health; having or showing good health.

> Wholesome foods are in this cabinet; junk foods are hidden here.

wily (WYE•lee) *adj.* Sly, cunning, crafty.

> In the forest, many wily animals are hunting their prey.

wither (WITH•ur) *v.* To lose moisture, dry up, and shrivel; to fade, lose freshness, wilt, and droop.

> Ms. Soares forgot to water her petunias, and they withered when she was on vacation.

wrath (RATH) *n.* Enormous anger, rage, and fury, often with a desire for revenge for a wrongdoing.

> I don't understand why Mr. Haimowitz feels such wrath toward me just because I dropped his computer.

zeal (ZEEL) *n.* Great enthusiasm for and eager devotion to a job, cause, ideal, goal, etc.

> Lourdes accomplished the difficult mission with hard work, energy, and gobs of zeal.

Index

Synonyms
  to avoid repetition, 122–123
  definition of, 118
  mini-thesaurus for, 124–135
  places to find, 121
  string of, 123–124
  for *very*, 136

T

Technology words, 19
Thesaurus
  alphabetical listing in, 119
  cross-references in, 119–120
  definition of, 118–119
  example of use of, 120–121
  how to use, 118–124
  parts of speech in, 122
  shades of meaning in,
    121–122
"True or false?" game, 147–148

V

Verb, 94
Vocabulary building
  games for, 142–154
  100 words for, 168–184
  techniques for, 138–140
  Web sites for, 116
Vocabulary words, used in
  context, 103

W

Web sites, for vocabulary
  building, 116
"Where in the world?" game,
  143–144
  answers to, 151–152
Word detective, 138
Word explorer, 138
Word families
  common, 95–98

parts of speech in, 94–95
Word history, 4–5
Word origins, 2–22
  answers to, 151–152
  from foreign languages,
    143–144
Words
  almost-rhyming, 15–16
  changing from place to
    place, 161–162
  changing over time,
    160–161
  combined, 17–19
  compound, 165
  confusing, 87–92
  context in meaning of,
    100–104
  double-sound, 16–17
  longest, 156–157
  made-up, 13–19
  with multi-language origins,
    5
  new, 19–22
  100 to learn, 168–184
  parts of, 24–61
  prefixes of, 24–33
  rhyming, 14–15
  roots of, 24, 34–50
  spelled-alike, 84–87 *See*
    Homographs
  suffixes of, 24, 50–60
  that sound alike, 64–84 *See*
    Homonyms
  tricky, 64–92
  using, 139–140

Marvin Terban has been described by *ALA Booklist* as "a master of children's wordplay" and by *School Library Journal* as a "nonfiction writer who captivates young people. . . . [He] excites children about language and challenges them to use it playfully and creatively." The Chelsea, Massachusetts, native has taught English for almost forty years at Columbia Grammar and Preparatory School on Manhattan's Upper West Side. He is the author of twenty-five titles on wordplay and language arts including *Checking Your Grammar, Scholastic Dictionary of Idioms, The Scholastic Dictionary of Spelling,* and *Punctuation Power.* He lives in New York with his wife, Karen, a special education teacher, and their two cats, Tiger and Peaches. The Terbans have two children, David, a computer digital artist, and Jennifer, a jewelry designer. In his free time, Terban speaks at schools across the country—and as far away as Japan.